Best Walks on Exmoor

Richard Webber

KU-042-005

Frances Lincoln

Frances Lincoln Ltd
4 Torriano Mews
Torriano Avenue
London NW5 2RZ
www.franceslincoln.com

British Library Cataloguing in Publication data
A catalogue record for this book is available from the British
Library

ISBN 978-0-7112-3287-7

9 8 7 6 5 4 3 2 1

Contents

The Best Walks

ACKNOWLEDGEMENTS

I would like to thank everyone who has helped during the writing and research of this book. My gratitude, as always, to my agent Jeffrey Simmons; everyone at Frances Lincoln; Clare O'Connor of Exmoor National Park's press office; John Clasby of Wessex Water for answering questions about the three Exmoor reservoirs mentioned in the book and Helen Calthrop-Owen at Satmap Systems Ltd (www.satmap.com; 0845 873 0101). Last, but by no means least, I'd like to thank Gregg Sparks for his company on Walks 2 and 12 and my wife, Paula, and children, Hollie and Peter, for their help, patience and company on several walks featured in the book. Finally, to anyone else who answered questions or offered advice, many thanks.

INTRODUCTION

There is nowhere quite like Exmoor. Although there are many beautiful regions in Britain, including Scotland's West Coast and its islands, the Yorkshire Dales and my beloved Lake District, Exmoor is a unique, unassuming corner of the United Kingdom which never fails to satisfy, excite or surprise the lucky visitors who explore its luscious landscapes.

Yes, call me biased if you like: after all, I grew up in the coastal town of Minehead, which lies on the edge of the National Park, and returned to the region some ten years ago. My affinity with Exmoor grew out of years spent walking, driving and picnicking in the many beauty spots this region boasts; now, with children of my own, I have the chance to show them the sheer majesty on offer right on their doorstep. And I'm pleased to say, they enjoyed accompanying me on some walks detailed within these covers.

So, let's consider a few vital statistics concerning Exmoor. Straddling the counties of Somerset and Devon, it was designated a National Park in 1954 and measures approximately 21 miles west to east and 15 miles north to south. It may be one of the smallest National Parks but what it lacks in size it makes up for in beauty and contrast, affording walkers a diverse landscape to explore.

Like its fictional heroine Lorna Doone, Exmoor is both wild and gentle. It's easy to see why author R.D. Blackmore chose it as the setting for his novel about a family of outlaws expelled from Scotland who came south and terrorised the locals. The scenery stirs the imagination, thanks to the coastline of stark cliffs lining the Bristol Channel, the wooded valleys, the tumbling streams and the wild, empty moors.

Fortunately, there are no large urban sites on Exmoor, with any settlements protected from over development. The lush landscape

– in places brushed by the influence of man, other corners pure unbridled wilderness – is punctuated by quaint villages, small towns and farms.

Exmoor has it all, and is so compact that it's easy to explore within the obligatory one-week or two-week holiday. But that's not all: weekenders can sample the delights of this region and return home refreshed and revitalised after a couple of days spent in the tranquillity of a rich, green landscape which, unlike other National Parks, ends abruptly at its northern edge on reaching precipitous cliffs – high, rugged hog's-backed monsters earning the coastline the accolade of possessing the highest sea cliffs in England and, in places, the remotest because in many spots there is no landward access for miles, thanks to the height and steepness of the cliffs.

Although Exmoor isn't devoid of bleakness and harsh landscapes – take a walk across The Chains in winter and you'll know what I mean – there is predominantly a cosiness and overriding softness in this part of the world, exemplified by the smooth, gentle curves of the hills and the soothing whispers of the myriad streams making their way to the open sea.

One of Exmoor's many plusses is that you don't have to endure a long, muscle-aching trek – unless you want to – to experience the region's cornucopia of landscapes: even a short, relaxing stroll can offer a rich tapestry of valleys, woods, pastures, moorlands and streams.

Considering my close links with Exmoor, you can understand why writing a walking book about this part of Britain has been pure joy; it's been a good reason – if ever I needed one – to pull on the walking boots and explore some of my favourite routes – all in the name of work!

Choosing thirty walks does, however, pose certain problems. Spreading out the Ordnance Survey map, it soon strikes you just how many walking routes exist on Exmoor. A plethora of green-dashed lines weave their way across the map, heading in every conceivable direction. So where do you start?

Countless walks could have been included so having to be selective has been a challenge. I could easily have picked routes thrice over. But a number of factors have been taken into account when choosing. For example, I've opted for circular rather than linear routes. Some starting points, of course, could be reached by public transport, but rural services can be infrequent with bus companies reviewing their route networks during these straitened times. So I've focused on using one's own transport to reach each starting point.

I've also tried to include some walks which haven't appeared in other walking books. Not only do I want to offer readers the chance to experience some of the region's lesser-known routes, but they're included because these are personal favourites. In contrast, some of those selected are obvious classics one expects to see in a walking book, such as Dunkery Beacon, the highest point not only on Exmoor but Somerset, too.

I don't know about you, but I like to pack a lot into a day, especially on holiday with just a week to see as much as possible of a particular region. Bearing this in mind, I've included a range of shorter walks which can be completed within half a day and, therefore, leave plenty of time to enjoy other activities.

If, like me, you're a keen walker but have a young family, you'll know that sometimes it's hard motivating a four-year-old to don walking boots – let alone partake in a lengthy hike. Distance and speed are key considerations when planning a walk for kiddies. I'm always on the look-out for routes which can be enjoyed by the whole family, regardless of age, and fortunately Exmoor throws up plenty of possibilities. So there are several in the book which provide the chance for a rewarding family walk.

And if that wasn't all, another consideration when selecting the routes was to include some relatively long walks. Of course, many people walk much further and I could have compiled an interesting batch of long-distance, all-day treks; that would have been fine, but what it wouldn't have achieved is variety; now, as Exmoor typifies variety in terms of its landscapes, I want this book to hold the same appeal: offering something for everyone.

ABOUT THIS BOOK

Maps

For each walk, I've drawn a sketch map to give an idea of the route covered. Bear in mind that they aren't drawn to scale and not intended to be used for the purpose of navigation. They just provide a visual overview of what you can expect and can be used alongside an Ordnance Survey map when initially sitting down to determine the route to be walked.

Virtually all Exmoor is covered by just one map: Ordnance Survey's Explorer OL9 map. In fact, it's only the very tip of the southern border which slips on to another sheet. But don't worry, you'll only need OL9 because it incorporates all thirty walks featured.

Many people might possess the pink OS Landranger map which, in its own right, is a very useful item. But with the scale of 1:50,000 (2 cm to 1 km) compared to the Explorer's 1: 25,000 (4 cm to 1 km), the latter is far superior for walking purposes: it's more detailed, covers more paths and tracks and is easier to use while trekking across the moors and along the valleys.

Directions

When detailing the directions for any given walk, I've tried to be as detailed yet concise as possible. I've avoided including too much description and additional information in the main body of each entry, preferring to put that within the introduction of each walk instead.

Nonetheless, the directions themselves are as informative and detailed as possible inasmuch as I've pointed out if a gate is wooden or metal, included the actual directions and distances shown on signposts, whether signposts are on the left or right of the path – details which could easily have been omitted but which, in my view, make it clearer when strolling along *in situ*.

What you'll notice is that when I last trod these routes, I noticed that, occasionally, waymarks had collapsed, signs were loose – these things happen. Farmers replace gates and fences which means that where a wooden five-bar gate once stood, there may now be a metal version. And that's not all: footpaths are occasionally diverted, perhaps because erosion has forced local authorities to re-direct walkers in order to prevent the condition worsening and to aid recovery. So, just as the make-up of the general landscape changes over time, so do these little details; bear this in mind if, hopefully, in years to come you're still using this book as a guide to some of the best walks on Exmoor.

Open Access land

The orange OS Explorer maps show the areas of open countryside and registered common land that have been categorised as Open Access land. Such areas have a lemon-coloured background and are unmistakable when spreading the map out in front of you.

It was the Countryside and Rights of Way Act 2000 for England and Wales which introduced such areas, providing sections of mountain, moor and heath where walkers are free to venture off the paths. People had campaigned for decades for such rights and, finally, in October 2005 they celebrated when over a million and a half hectares were opened up for people to enjoy.

It has to be pointed out, however, that people must be responsible when venturing on to Open Access land. Dog owners, for example, must keeps dogs on a lead not exceeding 2 m long between 1 March and 31 July, the primary breeding period for ground-nesting birds, or at any time of year when near livestock. But such conditions don't just apply to dog owners: anyone wandering on to Open Access land, like any part of the countryside, needs to act responsibly. For details of the Countryside Code for England and Wales, visit Natural England's website (www.naturalengland.org.uk) or phone 0845 600 3078.

Signs

There are always exceptions, of course, but in general there is excellent signage across Exmoor. Paths are not only generally well maintained but signs are well placed and clearly marked; the National Park, however, does take particular care in ensuring a balance is maintained between signing and the landscape. Signs are usually wooden and kept as small as possible in order to detract from the aesthetic beauty of the surroundings.

Signs, waymarks and, occasionally, other objects, such as tree trunks, are coloured-coded according to their classification. While public footpaths are yellow and public bridleways blue, restricted byways are purple and byways open to all traffic red.

Several long-distance walks cross Exmoor, too, and some are recognised and signed accordingly. The South West Coast Path is indicated, like all National Trails, by an acorn symbol, the Tarka Trail by a paw print, the Two Moors Way regional route by 'MW', the Coleridge Way regional route by a quill, and the Macmillan Way West by a 'MAC' symbol. Brief details of the long-distance routes follow.

Long-distance walking routes crossing Exmoor

SOUTH WEST COAST PATH

The 1,014-km (630-mile) South West Coast Path is the longest National Trail. Beginning in Minehead, it travels around the coast to the Dorset coastal town of Poole.

THE COLERIDGE WAY

Named after the Romantic poet, Samuel Taylor Coleridge, it's a 58-km (36-mile) walk from Nether Stowey – where the poet lived for a time – across the Quantock Hills, Brendon Hills and Exmoor, ending in the village of Porlock.

MACMILLAN WAY WEST

This 160-km (100-mile) plus branch path runs from the

Somerset market town of Castle Cary to Barnstaple, North Devon. It's just one of a series of long-distance paths promoted to raise money for the charity, Macmillan Cancer Relief.

TWO MOORS WAY

This 163-km (102-mile) route connects Ivybridge on the southern edge of Dartmoor with the picturesque town of Lynmouth, on the rugged Exmoor coast.

EXE VALLEY WAY

Covering around 72 km (45 miles), this is largely a river valley walk. It follows the Exe from its source to the sea along a pretty valley, passing through, among others, Dulverton, Bampton, Tiverton and Exeter.

TARKA TRAIL

Originally established in 1987, the trail covers some 290 km (180 miles) of paths taken by Tarka, the otter who was the subject of Henry Williamson's classic 1920s novel.

THE SAMARITANS WAY SOUTH WEST

Running from the Clifton Suspension Bridge in Bristol to Lynton, this route covers 160 km (100 miles) and passes through the heart of Exmoor, including Exford and the Doone Valley.

Preparation

When out walking, whether on Exmoor, Dartmoor or any other location, there are important factors to consider. Many speak for themselves, of course, and are simply common sense, but just as a reminder . . .

MAP

Always make sure you carry an OS map and know how to use it.

COMPASS

A compass should accompany you on every walk, too. Again, make sure you know how to use it because you never known when the weather might close in.

SUITABLE CLOTHING

As we all know, the weather in the UK can be very unreliable – more so on high ground, such as Exmoor. Therefore, carry clothes for any eventuality, including waterproofs.

BOOTS

Always wear suitable boots which protect not only your foot but ankle, too. Plenty of tread is needed for grip.

MOBILE PHONE

I carry my mobile with me at all times while walking. Accidents can happen to the most experienced walkers and having a means of contacting family, friends or emergency services can be a lifeline.

SATELLITE NAVIGATION SYSTEMS

Satnav systems can be extremely useful for pinpoint accuracy when establishing your exact position; they have many other uses, too, including planning a route by adding waymarks and showing that you're keeping to it, providing data about your route – the list is endless. However, they run by batteries so make sure you have back ups. I always say that a satnav system should complement the OS map and compass, not replace it.

CONSIDER ROUTE

Think about the route you're taking before setting off and consider what – if any – challenges you might meet along the way.

COUNTRYSIDE CODE
Respect the Countryside Code.

Exmoor in a nutshell

- We have the sedimentary rock and the effects of the Ice Age to largely thank for Exmoor's predominantly smooth curves and gentle rolling moorland.
- The National Park covers an area of 694 square km.
- Exmoor boasts 55 km (34 miles) of coastline.
- There are 208 scheduled ancient monuments.
- The park contains sixteen conservation areas.
- Around 1.5 million people visit most years, fewer than in most other National Parks. This, however, makes for a quieter, less spoilt and less crowded environment.

The A39 main road runs from Bath to Cornwall's south coast, cutting across the northern strip of Exmoor in the process. It climbs the notoriously steep Porlock Hill – ascending 400 m (1,300 feet) in less than two miles – and continues towards County Gate, where the counties of Somerset and Devon meet.

Back in January 1899, the stretch of road from Porlock to Lynmouth, further down the coast, witnessed a monumental effort by a group of men and horses during a raging storm. The event, known as the Overland Launch, unfolded as a severe storm battered the region.

A casualty of the rough seas was the 1,900-ton, fully rigged vessel, *Forrest Hall*, which foundered off Porlock. The sheer force of the wind had already destroyed a pier at nearby Woody Bay, so it's no surprise that Lynmouth's lifeboat was prevented from launching.

Desperate to help the stricken vessel's crew, the relatively sheltered waters at Porlock Weir, some 13 miles away, offered an opportunity. So the lifeboat was dragged and pushed up Countisbury Hill, across Exmoor and down Porlock Hill to the weir, finally launching twelve hours later. Thankfully, these unbelievable endeavours were rewarded and the lifeboat crew were able to shepherd the cargo vessel to a safe haven.

Today, the Lynmouth–Porlock road is one of the most scenic I've ever driven. There are also plenty of varied, interesting walks on offer both sides of the road; this jaunt is one of my favourites in this corner of Exmoor, partly because it epitomises the contrasts this national park affords walkers: sea views, rugged coastline, open heathland, hidden valleys, varied woodland and pastures, all blending to create the region's rich landscape.

Beginning near the top of Porlock Hill, the route heads north initially before running along the side of the hill amid fine coastal

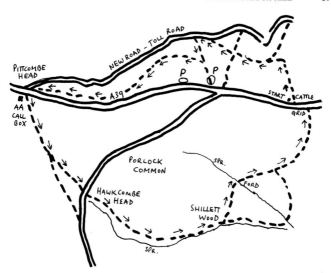

views; eventually, you cross the A39 at the site of an old AA call box, which is, in fact, a listed building. Box 137's claim to fame is that during the devastating Lynmouth Flood Disaster in 1952, heroic policeman Derek Harper used the phone to alert headquarters of the tragic events unfolding.

Once this side of the road, the route eventually drops into a steep-sided valley and Shillett Wood – one of the non-intervention areas of Hawkcombe Wood National Nature Reserve – before climbing back to meet the A39 once again. A wonderful little walk.

Distance: 6.5 km/4 miles approx | Time: 2 hours approx. (with children) | Parking and starting point: Off-road parking near the top of Porlock Hill, on the right immediately after a cattle grid (grid ref: SS 865 460) | Toilets at start: None | Difficulties: No particular difficulties, although on the second half of the walk the path descends into Shillett Wood, leaving a short climb back to your car on the final leg | Map: Explorer map OL9

THE WALK

From your car, walk away from the road, following the wide track in the direction of 'Public bridleway 1½ West Porlock'. Straight away, you're treated to some sumptuous views, like the one greeting you now on the right, down across Porlock Bay to the jagged, rocky headland of Hurlstone Point.

The track gently turns to the left, drops briefly and bends further to the left. Ahead you catch a glimpse of farms, including Eastcott, and the Toll Road, labelled the 'New Road' on the OS map. This tarmaced road, owned by Porlock Manor Estate, offers a scenic and less daunting route to the top of the hill, avoiding the hairpin bends and 1 in 4 gradient of Porlock Hill. Constructed in the mid-nineteenth century, the Toll Road is 7.25 km (4½ miles) long, running from Porlock to Pittcombe Head.

Ignore a grassy West Porlock-bound track dropping on the right, close to an iron gate; our path – deep rutted in places – continues bending left as it weaves its way along the side of the hill. Although never far from the A39, the road and cars remain out of sight. The path is predominantly level, which is just as well because you don't want any distractions because you'll constantly be looking right, across the fields and Bristol Channel towards the South Wales' coastline.

Soon, you'll join a wide, stony track coming down the side of the hill on your left. Turn right on joining it and continue until reaching the tarmaced Toll Road. Turn left and walk up, passing the entrance to Eastcott Farm on the right. When you see a wooden signpost on the right, turn left, signed 'Public footpath Whitstones Post'.

The path – not the clearest in places – climbs through gorse bushes and bends left. Keep your eyes peeled for a smaller path on the right, cutting back sharply. When you spot it, take it. On your right, you'll see Westcott Farm and the trees of Westcott Brake, while the stunted hawthorns punctuating the landscape are ideal when framing the many photos you're likely to take during this walk.

Looking north, down over a heather-clad hillside from the A39 atop Porlock Hill

The path climbs, but just before reaching the A39, look carefully for a small path heading off to the right, through heather – it's easily missed. You'll see the Toll Road to your right and the main road to your left, just up over the bank. If you miss the turning and hit the A39, don't worry. Just turn right on to the road, taking great care because it's busy, and join the path further along. Alternatively, walk along the side of the road until reaching the old AA box, on your left.

Back on the path, you might see Exmoor ponies roaming the hillside. The route cuts through tracts of heather, meeting a grassy pull-in, just before the Toll Road joins the A39. At the road junction, cross to the black and yellow AA call box before turning left and walking a few metres back along the road in the direction of Porlock until, on your right, you'll see a stony pull-in by a metal

gate. Follow the wide, rubbly track leading from this area, running close to a fence on your right.

Before reaching the end of the track, opposite a wooden five-bar gate and large rocks on the right, turn by small trees to a lay-by on the Exford-bound road which cuts across Porlock Common.

Cross the road to a wooden post at Hawkcombe Head, indicating you're joining a public bridleway to Porlock, 5.5 km (3½ miles) away. Ignore the path rising to the left from the post and take the route which descends and becomes a narrow track running alongside a spring on your right. The path clings to the side of the heather-clad valley, gradually entering Shillett Wood.

It's a pretty wood, with a carpet of whortleberry bushes and an array of trees, including a fine display of stunted sessile oaks last coppiced around ninety years ago. Owned by the National Park since 1965, this ancient woodland boasts around 182 species of lichen growing on its trees and is also of great importance for mosses and fungi.

On the left, you'll eventually notice a fence, and as some water trickles into the main flow from the left, you need to cross – looking out for the blue bridleway mark on the tree. The path weaves its way down through Shillett Wood with a fence on the left, water to the right.

Soon, you'll approach a wooden fence and two gates. Cross the stream on the left and walk towards the smaller wooden five-bar gate. Go through, and on joining a stony track you're faced with three possible routes. The right-hand option winds up to Bromham Farm, the middle slips down to Porlock, so we need the left-hand route: climbing through trees, this wide track is used by forestry and farm vehicles.

Reaching a split, ignore the right-hand track and follow the blue sign, across water; ignore a path immediately on the right and climb the steep track up through trees. Soon, you'll catch a glimpse of Bromham Farm on your right. Pass a small path on the left while continuing to a wooden sign at the end of the steep

The famous AA call box 137, now a listed building, at Pittcombe Head

LEFT *Walking through Shillett Wood*
ABOVE *Walking on top Porlock Hill with Hurlstone Point providing a perfect backdrop*

climb. Follow in the direction of 'Bridleway Porlock Hill (A39)', over the cattle grid and around the lower part of a field.

To your right, the cairn atop Dunkery Beacon stands out against the skyline. Pass a barn on the left, while ahead are splendid views towards Hurlstone Point, North Hill and the Bristol Channel. Over another cattle grid and you'll reach the A39. Turn left and walk up the hill, taking care on the road. After approximately 90 m (100 yards) on your right, beside another cattle grid, you'll see your car.

DID YOU KNOW?

- It's claimed that whortleberries – or bilberries as they're also commonly known and which grow in abundance on Exmoor – had their uses during the Second World War. The berries became popular with RAF pilots who believed they improved their vision during nightime bombing raids.
- Drivers are advised – quite rightly – to descend Porlock Hill in low gear but some still prefer to go a little faster, relying heavily on their brakes. The result is the occasional smell of rubber lingering at the bottom of the hill.

County Gate – Doone Valley

This varied walk heads into the heart of Lorna Doone country, following Badgworthy Water, which runs to the sea through a lovely, tranquil valley. This is true Doone Country, with Badgworthy Valley itself being the main setting for the 1860s book, written by novelist R.D. Blackmore. Thanks to Blackmore's famous novel, many settings used have long been a draw for tourists – in fact, such is this region's association with his writing that Doone Country is even mentioned on Ordnance Survey's Explorer map.

The walk begins at County Gate, situated on the A39 at the Somerset/Devon border. Here, a café-cum-information centre is located in an eighteenth-century building which once served as a staging post for the horse-drawn coaches travelling on this then turnpike road.

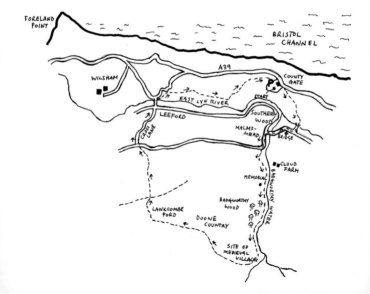

From the car park, you drop into a deep valley before reaching the quaint village of Malmsmead where, among other attractions, a campsite and beautiful tea gardens can be found. From here, the walk into Badgworthy 'Doone' Valley begins in earnest, passing a memorial stone for Blackmore along the way: it was placed here by the Lorna Doone Centenary Committee in 1969.

The delights of this route continue all the way back to the car, including crossing the open expanse of Brendon Common and dropping into the pretty village of Brendon before climbing back to the car park at County Gate.

Just ensure your well-thumbed volume of *Lorna Doone* is packed into your rucksack alongside your Ordnance Survey map and, of course, this book!

Distance: 14.5 km/9 miles approx. | Time: 4 hours approx. | Parking and starting point: Free car park at County Gate on the A39, between Porlock and Lynmouth (grid ref: SS 793 486) | Toilets at start: At the car park | Difficulties: The route has many ascents and descents and is strenuous in places | Map: Explorer map OL9

THE WALK

Leaving the car at County Gate car park, head towards the main road before slipping through a five-bar gate on your right, following the sign marked 'Bridleway to Malmsmead, Doone Valley and Oare'.

The path hugs a fence as it drops into a valley, with views ahead of the Doone Valley Campsite and hills behind. When you reach the valley bottom, bend right, following 'Bridleway Malmesmead ⅓'.

Cross the footbridge at Oare Water and go through a five-bar gate. Trace the path by some barns and through a metal gate, marking the entrance to Parsonage Farm.

On meeting the road, turn right. Walk by the entrance to

Cloud Farm and over a stone bridge, passing The Buttery café and gift shop on your right. Turn immediately left, signed 'Lane leading to public footpath – Doone Valley'.

The road climbs for around 450 m (490 yards). Make sure you turn around and admire the views back towards County Gate before taking the wide track on your left, close to a bend. Go through the five-bar gate signed 'Public bridleway Badgworthy Valley ½'.

The path turns to the left. When faced with two gates, pick the right-hand option. You'll stay tight to the stony bank before going through a metal gate and over a stream.

Ignore a footbridge on your left for Cloud Farm campsite. Walk straight on, signed 'Bridleway Doone Valley'. The path travels up the valley, to the right of Badgworthy Water, passing the memorial stone, on your right, dedicated to Richard Blackmore.

At a split, keep right – don't turn off. You'll enter a stunted oak wood. Keep straight ahead, going through a five-bar gate. You'll pass a wooden post on the left, marked 'Sir Hugh's Ride' (apparently named after Sir Hugh Stuckley of the Badgworthy Land Company). When three paths converge, carry on, following the river.

Crossing a footbridge, your route makes its way to the head of the valley, finally leaving the woods behind.

On the left, at the confluence of rivers, you'll see the remains of the medieval village of Badgworthy, which it's believed was the original inspiration for Blackmore's famous novel. It's an ideal spot for opening the flask and sandwich box. Once replete, at the crossroads of paths, carry on ahead. Soon, the path bends right, passing a blue-marked rock and post indicating 'Brendon Common'.

The grassy path keeps left of a stony bank as it climbs on to the open expanse of Brendon Common. It becomes imperceptible at times, too. At a split, keep right and enjoy the gentle climb over the Common before reaching a fence and metal gate.

Keep straight ahead, following the bridleway sign. Up here, a region inhabited by Exmoor ponies, you can see for miles on a

Looking south from County Gate, with Lorna Doone Farm campsite visible

clear day. To your right, that view includes the Welsh coast and in the far distance the peaks of the Brecon Beacons.

The path sweeps around and descends to Lankcombe Ford before rising again, up to Tippacott Ridge. At a signpost, go straight across at the crossroads of paths, signed 'Bridleway Brendon 2'.

In front of you, expansive views back towards County Gate, the Bristol Channel and the Welsh coast will have you reaching for your camera.

At the next sign, stay on the bridleway to Brendon. When the path joins a road, cross and go over a cattle grid, heading for Brendon, 1.6 km (1 mile away) at the sign named Cross Gate.

Walk along the road. As it bends, you'll be afforded charming views of the villages of Brendon and Leeford below. Arriving in Brendon, go straight across at the junction, for Lynmouth, Lynton and Porlock. Once over the road bridge, turn right, signposted 'Porlock light vehicles', and go up the road, climbing gradually.

Reaching Hall Farm on the right, look for the 'Public Footpath – County Gate 2' sign. Climb up the wooden steps; the path begins to rise and bends right.

A memorial stone for Richard Blackmore, author of Lorna Doone, close to Badgworthy Water

Go through a gate and carry on ahead, with fields to your left and a valley right. Through another gate and begin a steep climb. Eventually the path drops before passing through a five-bar gate.

After a stepped stile the route traverses a field. Cross a small footbridge and turn left, uphill, before the path bends to the right.

Continue to a signpost, following the County Gate path. After a small gate, keep left at a split, signed 'County Gate Visitor Centre'. The car park now appears on the skyline, so continue back to your car.

DID YOU KNOW?

- R.D. Blackmore's family originated from the North Devon village of Parracombe. His grandfather, meanwhile, was rector at Oare in the nineteenth century.
- The church in the village of Brendon was moved from nearby Cheriton during the eighteenth century.

BELOW *Looking down on the villages of Leeford and Brendon*
OVERLEAF *The open landscape of Doone Country, heading away from Doone Valley*

Wherever you travel in the UK, there is an endless supply of outstanding views and landscapes – that's part of what makes Britain so beautiful. I've been lucky enough to experience many first hand but none, in my opinion, is as awe-inspiring as what greets you on this walk.

In fact, as soon as you step out the car you're treated to a wonderful vista, down across Porlock Bay and along a rugged coastline boasting headlands galore. Moorland, woodland, coastline, combes, picturesque villages – this walk has them all.

The lion's share of the route offers panoramic views, so don't be surprised if you take longer than the estimated time. Don't hurry, take time to savour this gilt-edged walk.

Although the route doesn't descend to Bossington Beach, you'll hear the draw of the water against the steep-shelving pebbled ridge sweeping around Porlock Bay. It's a sound which will remain with you for some while as you head towards Allerford.

The village of Allerford is mentioned in the Domesday Book and is a tranquil spot. One of its highlights and, arguably, the most famous is the delightful eighteenth-century packhorse bridge, crossing the River Aller. Such bridges were constructed to enable pack animals, laden with goods, to make a safe passage across rivers; many examples of such medieval bridges remain within Exmoor National Park.

The walk continues to Selworthy, a delightful spot designed to resemble an old-fashioned village by landowner Sir Thomas Acland. He used the cottages as accommodation for the aged and infirm from his Holnicote Estate, which covers 20 square miles of picturesque Exmoor landscape.

Before starting the steepest part of the walk, up through Selworthy Combe and back to the car park, you might be lucky

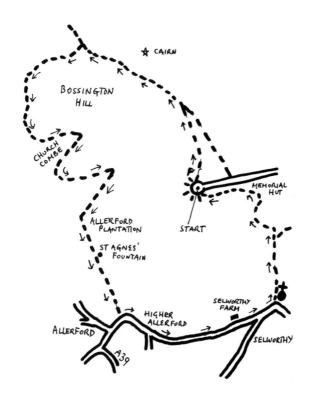

and catch the seasonal Periwinkle Cottage Tea Rooms open on Selworthy Green. Treat yourself to a cream tea!

Distance: | 8 km/5 miles approx. | Time: 2½ hours approx. | Parking and starting point: Car park at the end of North Hill (grid ref: SS 910 476). Free but National Trust box for contributions. | Toilets at start: None | Difficulties: Steep path up through Selworthy Combe to the car park on the last leg of the walk | Map: Explorer map OL9

THE WALK

From the car park, walk along the wide path signed 'Bossington Hill and Coast Path' which heads towards the cairn atop Bossington Hill and Hurlstone Point beyond.

After around five minutes, a track joins from the right but continue until you reach a signpost. While 'Lynch Combe' is signed left, go straight on, marked 'Coast Path'.

Delight in the beautiful vistas all around: across to the South Wales coast, down the undulating rocky coastline and the rural landscape towards Dunkery Beacon, the highest point on Exmoor.

After the wooden waymark carrying the acorn symbol, the path gradually descends to a signpost. Bear left, for 'Coast Path – Porlock'.

The path slips further down the hill to another sign. Here, it's worth making a short detour. Follow the track to your right,

Bossington and Porlock from the side of Bossington Hill

beginning by a wooden bench. After a few minutes, you'll be above Hurlstone Point, home to the remains of an old coastguard station, built in the early 1900s and operational until 1983.

After experiencing the beauty of your immediate surroundings, retrace your steps to the wooden bench and at the signpost, take the path ahead for 'Lynch Combe'.

There are more views of pebbly Bossington Beach, Porlock Bay, the villages of Bossington and Porlock and Dunkery Hill forming a perfect backdrop as you follow the path around the hill. Reaching steep-sided Church Combe, follow the contour line of the land. You'll lose the views for a time on entering heavily-wooded Allerford Plantation, but on warm days the shade is most welcome.

At a junction of paths, veer right, for Allerford. After around 15 m (17 yards), go through the wooden gate and head for 'St Agnes' Fountain/Allerford'. Keep on this path down through the woods, ignoring two tracks on your left running back up to North Hill.

Bossington Beach and Porlock Bay from the side of Bossington Hill

Looking across Selworthy Church's cemetery towards Dunkery Hill

When you reach a junction offering the choice of six routes, you've arrived at St Agnes' Fountain. Sit on the substantial wooden seat and rest your legs for a while, relaxing to the sound of running water.

The blink-and-you'll-miss-it St Agnes' Fountain may be nothing more than a trickle on the edge of a path but is of interest because it's believed to have been named after the youngest daughter of Sir Thomas Acland, who owned much land in this area.

At the six-path junction, turn left and immediately right for Allerford and continue through the woods. At the next junction, where one path bends sharp right and another climbs to the left, pick the middle option and descend to two gates.

Passing through both gates, follow the path crossing a field and through another gate to a narrow road, marking your arrival in Allerford. Turn right and cross the bridge to explore the quiet village.

After, retrace your steps over the bridge and up the narrow road, bending right. At Jasmine Cottage, a thatched property on the left, keep walking ahead, joining a stony track edged by tall hedgerows.

The eighteenth-century packhorse bridge in Allerford

Keep on the track, which has occasional splendid views across fields to Dunkery, until reaching a tarmac road, signifying you've arrived at the village of Selworthy. Past some farm buildings, you'll reach another road. Turn left.

After the public toilets on the left, look for a wooden gate immediately on your left. Enter and walk up to Selworthy Green, a picturesque setting with a cluster of lemon-painted thatched cottages and the welcome Periwinkle Cottage Tea Rooms, serving traditional cream teas, assorted cakes and snacks.

Follow the path skirting the green, past the National Trust shop, through the gate at the war memorial and take a look at the white lime-washed fourteenth-century Selworthy Church, before returning to the war memorial and turning right up a track, signed 'Public bridleway to Selworthy Beacon'.

The path leads into Selworthy Combe. At the next signpost, veer right, continuing in the direction of the beacon. You need to branch left at the next sign, again for the beacon. You're likely to

Looking across the fields to Dunkery from a track between Allerford and Selworthy

TOP *Periwinkle Cottage Tea Rooms at Selworthy Green*
ABOVE *Selworthy Church*
RIGHT *A thatched cottage at Selworthy*

be entertained by the sound of birdsong as you climb through the woods.

Before long, the path emerges from the woods and skirts the trees. Just before reaching a road, turn left to a weather hut, erected in remembrance of Sir Thomas Acland in 1878 at a spot selected by his then youngest surviving son. Follow the 'Easy Access Path' snaking its way through the trees to your car.

DID YOU KNOW?

- The village of Allerford was the childhood home of Admiral John Moresby who, in the 1870s, explored New Guinea and ended up having the capital city, Port Moresby, named after him. If it's open, pop into the West Somerset Rural Life Museum, in the old school house, which also boasts a mock Victorian classroom.
- The village of Selworthy, particularly the lemon-washed houses bordering the green, was rebuilt by Sir Thomas Acland in 1828.

WALK 4:   *Bossington, extending to Porlock Weir*

This walk begins in Bossington, a beautiful hamlet full of olde worlde cottages. Many are built of stone, thatch and cob with tall distinctive chimneys and flowers adorning the facades. Some of the dwellings still possess bread ovens with their tall round chimneys reaching sufficient height to take any sparks away from the thatch.

Among Bossington's many other attractions is Kitnor's Tea Room and Garden, selling the obligatory cream teas, homemade cakes and other fine offerings.

It's from the nearby car park that this walk begins, crossing Horner Water, which is on its final stage of an 8-mile journey to the sea at Bossington Beach. You turn towards the sea and walk around the foot of Bossington Hill before reaching the distinctive beach, a shingle bar extending around the bay to Porlock Weir.

The route comes off the beach and returns to the hamlet but can be extended to Porlock Weir. The extension takes you around a marsh area carpeted in wild plants, including glasswort and yellow-horned poppies, and frequented by a host of different birds, such as lapwing.

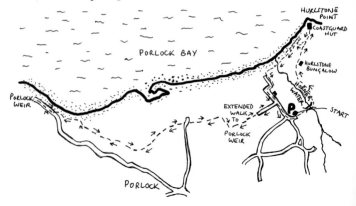

Cottages at Bossington

In the past, stopping the sea breaching the shingle ridge was a priority but nothing could prevent waters rushing through during a storm in 1996, leaving a state of flood behind. But nature took its course and a precious saltmarsh began to form, providing a delicate habitat for, among others, plants and birds.

So whether you decide to keep it short or fancy the extension, you'll be rewarded with fine walks and striking scenery.

Distance: 3.25 km/2 miles approx., but if you extend the walk to Porlock Weir, add a further 4.5 km/2¾ miles each way | Time: 1 hour approx. (with children) for the shorter walk | Parking and starting point: The National Trust pay-and-display car park (free for members) in Bossington. Look out for the red phone box at the entrance (grid ref: SS 897 480) | Toilets at start: At the car park | Difficulties: Generally an easy walk with no particular difficulties, although it's hard work trudging along Bossington Beach | Map: Explorer map OL9

THE WALK

From the car park, follow the sign for 'Public bridleway Hurlstone ¾' and cross the wooden bridge. Turn left, signed 'Coast path and bridleway Hurlstone Point', with Horner Water on your left.

The wide stony track bends right, leaving the water's edge, and begins to rise as it runs around the base of Bossington Hill.

The route takes you through trees and passes Hurlstone Bungalow, a green wooden dwelling, on the right. When the path splits to two five-bar gates, keep right and go through. The path climbs steadily, levels and rises again before bending right.

Leaving the trees behind, enjoy a fine view up over the side of Bossington Hill on the right and across Porlock Bay on the left. You'll pass a National Trust collection box and a wooden bench on your right, at a junction of paths – continue ahead.

When the path splits, make a quick detour by continuing straight on (the path climbs) to the abandoned coastguard hut at Hurlstone Point. Soon, a path joins from the right: after bending to the left, you'll reach steps leading up to the hut; it was built in the early 1900s but, sadly, decommissioned in 1983. The hut commands uninterrupted views across the Bristol Channel to the Welsh coast and along the spectacular Somerset and North Devon coastline.

Now it's time to retrace your steps. At the first junction, keep right and take the next turning right and go over a stile. The land drops away steeply on your left as the narrow path winds its way down to Bossington Beach.

The pebble beach is, in fact, a steep-shelving shingle bar and our route runs along towards Porlock Weir, in the distance. It's slow going over the pebbles. Look out for any remains of ruined buildings: lime kilns existed here. Limestone shipped in from South Wales across the channel was burnt and used locally for fertiliser, lime wash for cottages and other purposes.

Eventually, you'll reach wooden posts on the pebbles before a Second World War pillbox. Turn left and follow a track past a red

The shingle ridge of Bossington Beach

'Bathing Dangerous' sign, leading away from Bossington Beach. It twists and turns, passing Bossington Pumping Station on the left, with views across to Porlock on the right: the spire of the Church of St Dubricius, a Grade I listed building, is prominent.

Reaching a wooden sign on the right at a junction, carry on for Bossington/Minehead. Before you do, however, note that the sign pointing right is marked 'Coast Path Porlock Weir via marsh': this is the route to follow if you want to extend the walk, as detailed shortly.

Heading back to your car, you'll reach the first of the quaint yellow-painted thatched cottages on the right, with a brook running along.

The road splits with a sign showing 'Porlock 1', pointing right. Continue around the bend – with the brook remaining on your right – back to the car park on the left.

As mentioned, if you want to extend the walk, why not continue to Porlock Weir? At the point where you reached the wooden sign on the right at a junction, turn on to the South West Coast Path, signified by the acorn symbol.

Cottages at Porlock Weir

For 4.5 km (2¾ miles), the South West Coast Path makes its way across agricultural land that, at times, resembles a lagoon as water seeps through the steeply-shelving bar across Bossington Beach. You're following the coast path until you reach the B3225, running from Porlock village to the weir.

After climbing steps on to the road, turn right and walk along the road to the weir, perhaps stopping for a drink or bite to eat at the Ship Inn. Don't forget to explore the hamlet of Porlock Weir, once a busy port and now popular for local yachts and fishing boats. In the eighteenth and nineteenth centuries, coal was the primary cargo arriving at the harbour, having been shipped from South Wales. But the port's existence dates back some 1,000 years while some of the cottages in this tiny settlement were built in the seventeenth century.

To return to your car, walk back along the B3225 and climb

down the steps, following in the direction of the sign for 'Coast Path Bossington 2¾ via marsh'.

DID YOU KNOW?

- Much birdlife and maritime flowers can be spotted while walking from Bossington Beach to Porlock Weir. Look out for little egrets and skylarks on the bird front and, among others, yellow horned poppies when it comes to flora.

- In the 1850s, a ketch named *Lizzie* sank off Gore Point, just around the coast from Porlock Weir. She'd ran into trouble off Lynmouth during a storm and her crew were rescued. When the storm subsided, the captain plus a fresh crew returned to the craft in an attempt to salvage it. But, sadly, it sank and its remains lie submerged off the Point.

Horner is a quiet, restful hamlet 5 miles south-west of Minehead and 3 south-east of Porlock, near Exmoor's northern border. All around are trees and hills and, in addition to the fine scenery and walking opportunities, there is much to draw people.

Children, for example, love paddling and throwing sticks into Horner Water as it runs through the hamlet while there are also two tea gardens to choose from, my favourite being the Horner Tea Garden. Many people rate the cream teas among the best they've tasted. I can certainly vouch for the homemade Victoria sandwich – definitely the best I've sampled.

This area of Exmoor is a Site of Special Scientific Interest. Horner Wood, which cloaks more than 800 acres of moorland, is home to hundreds of species of lichen and fungi, many archaeological features and an abundance of insects and birds, including wood warblers, redstarts and dippers. But that's not all: in this ancient woodland, regarded among the most beautiful in England, live fourteen of the UK's sixteen species of bats.

The region is brimming over with interest; there are even remains of a medieval village hiding among the trees. The footings of six dwellings are still visible plus the ancient village street, now used as a bridleway.

But this is more than a walk through a dense ancient woodland – of which a substantial chunk is oak, making it one of the largest oak woodlands in Britain – because as soon as you start climbing around Crawter Hill and up to the route's highest point, above Horner Wood, you're greeted by impressive panoramic views. You can see across to Dunkery Beacon, back towards Bossington Hill and the Bristol Channel beyond, Porlock Hill . . . the list seems endless.

Beginning in the National Trust car park in the hamlet itself,

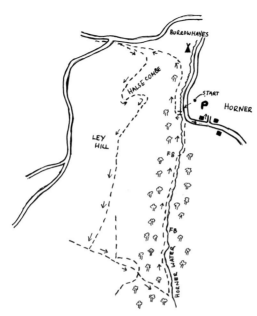

you join the Coleridge Way briefly (see 'Introduction' for details of this long-distance walk) before the path climbs on to open moorland, above the tree line of Horner Wood, affording walkers fine views before dropping, steeply in places to the valley bottom. After the muscle-testing descent, it's a welcome level stroll back to Horner and refreshments, following – for a time – Horner Water's journey towards the sea.

Distance: 6 km/3¾ miles approx. | Time: 2 hours approx. | Parking and starting point: National Trust car park in Horner. Free for members. Pay-and-display for non-members (grid ref: SS 898 454) | Toilets at start: In National Trust car park | Difficulties: No specific difficulties but the ascent and descent are steep in places, particularly down through trees in Horner Wood | Map: Explorer map OL9

THE WALK

Turn left out of the car park entrance. Around 23 m (25 yards) up the road, on the right, you'll see 'Hacketty Way' etched on a wooden sign for 'Public Bridleway Porlock'. Turn here and go over a footbridge, which is actually a seventeenth-century packhorse bridge.

The path bends right after the bridge and at the next sign, follow in the direction of 'Bridleway Luckbarrow', leading through the wood, with a stream to your right.

Go through a five-bar gate and the undulating path skirts around the back of Burrowhayes Farm, a caravan and campsite. Ignore any turnings on the left. At a wooden sign head for 'Porlock ¾'.

When the path splits, with the campsite and a field on your right, bear left, heading away from the fenced field boundary. You'll pass a batch of holly trees and will see a narrow tarmaced road, on your right. Just before the path meets the road, bend back on yourself and up a path on the left signed, 'Granny's Ride, Horner Wood', most likely dedicated to a member of the Acland Family.

After a steady climb up beyond the tree line, you'll emerge into the open with fine views on your left, across fields to Periton Hill and Wootton Common, and the unmistakable white church at Selworthy in view, too.

When a path crosses your route at a yellow-marked post, carry on. The path bends to the left, crosses a stream in steep-sided Halse Combe and climbs to a wooden sign, indicating three routes. Rather than continue on Granny's Ride, climb uphill on the steep right-hand route, signed, 'Ley Hill'.

On reaching a crossroads of paths, go straight on. Ignore any side routes and remain on the main track. Eventually, you'll meet another path, joining from the right. Here, the land levels out, giving chance for your muscles to recuperate!

The wide track bends gently to the right. Ignore another

The route to Ley Hill, above Horner, with Bossington Hill and North Hill in the background

large track on the right. Around 100 yards later, at a junction of paths, turn left towards dense woodland with Dunkery Hill providing a perfect backdrop.

The track enters Horner Wood and at a wooden sign (broken when I completed the walk), follow in the direction of Horner Combe. Almost immediately, the path splits and you'll need to follow the middle option which, shortly, is signed for 'Horner Water'.

At the next wooden sign, with Granny's Ride signed left and right, continue straight down. At times, the path isn't the easiest or clearest to navigate – especially when leaves carpet the floor – as it bends slightly to the right before carrying on down through the dense woodland.

Treading carefully, you'll eventually exit the steep and wooded descent and meet a wide track. Turn left, with Horner Water running along on your right. Continue ahead, ignoring a path and footbridge across the water on your right. In fact, you'll keep the water on your right-hand side virtually the entire way along

An Exmoor pony rests on Ley Hill, above Horner

the track. Go through a wooden five-bar gate before the path bends to the right, over a stone bridge, and turns left towards cottages, indicating you're arriving back in Horner.

On reaching a road, turn right, walking past a row of quaint cottages. Make sure you leave enough time to take a well-earned break at Horner Tea Garden (usually open March–October), the last dwelling, just before a gated path leading into the car park.

This is the quintessential English tea garden, sited within the grounds of a Grade II listed building amid beautiful surroundings. Not to be missed, especially as you can partake in a little ornithology: while sinking your teeth into another scone or slice of cake, tiny birds may swoop to your table, hoping to pick up a crumb or two.

Once you've satisfied your tastebuds, leave the tea garden through the wooden gate, turn left (be careful, because you're stepping out on to a narrow road) and immediately left through another gate. The short path leads back to the car park where you left your vehicle.

Walking into Horner Wood, just before descending to Horner Water

Cottages at Horner

DID YOU KNOW?
- The silver-washed fritillary butterfly breeds in Horner Wood and feeds on violets.
- Just up the road from the Horner Tea Garden is an impressive water mill. Now a residential property, it was built in the 1850s for a local miller. The business closed its doors before the Second World War.

No walking book on Exmoor is complete without a visit to Dunkery Beacon, the highest point in the National Park – and in Somerset, for that matter. Standing just over 518 m (1,700 feet) above sea level, it should be on everyone's itinerary when visiting this part of the world.

Pick summertime for your visit and Dunkery Hill looks resplendent with its cloak of purple heather, but any time of year is special – even on a blustery winter's day it has an unmistakable quality. Owned by the National Trust and classed as a nature reserve, the surrounding moorland supports many forms of fauna, including red deer, Exmoor ponies and even the merlin, the UK's smallest bird of prey.

In days gone by, Dunkery Beacon was used as a fire signal station. Since prehistoric times, hilltops such as Dunkery's were used not only for keeping watch for potential invaders but passing on warnings by setting beacons alight.

I'll never forget June 1977 and the Queen's Silver Jubilee. With my family, I joined the throngs of people making their way to the top of North Hill, overlooking the coastal town of Minehead. The Queen lit a bonfire beacon at Windsor Castle, triggering the lighting of beacons across the UK. One of those was Selworthy Beacon at the end of North Hill and I remember glancing across and seeing Dunkery ablaze, too. A truly memorable occasion.

There are various ways to reach the summit of Dunkery Hill and some might regard my suggestion as a rather circuitous route to the beacon, our ultimate goal on this walk. But to me, it's worth deviating a little by heading away from our target just to wander and enjoy the sparkling scenery along a route known as the Dunster Path; you won't be disappointed.

The walk begins at Webber's Post, a wonderful spot with views

An Exmoor pony near Horner

up over Horner Wood towards the open landscapes atop Porlock Hill. It's thought to be named after a local hunting enthusiast, Tom Webber, who chose this vantage point as the ideal location for watching his hounds in the valley below.

After just over a mile on the aforementioned Dunster Path, heading eastwards, the route connects to the Macmillan Way West, a fully waymarked path off the main Macmillan Way (see 'Introduction' for details of this long-distance walk). It takes you back in a south-westerly direction all the way to Dunkery Beacon and beyond. We leave the long-distance trail at the beacon, returning to our car around the lower slopes of Dunkery Hill. It's a beautiful walk.

Distance: 9.75 km/6 miles approx. | Time: 2½ hours approx. | Parking and starting point: Free parking at Webber's Post, on the slopes of Dunkery Hill (grid ref: SS 902 438) | Toilets at start: None | Difficulties: The stretch of walk taking you on the Macmillan Way West is a steady ascent to the beacon, but, overall, it's not a particularly challenging walk | Map: Explorer map OL9

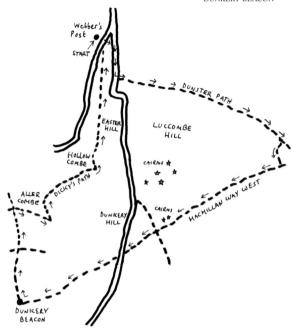

THE WALK

From the rough-surfaced car park at Webber's Post, walk across a narrow tarmaced road leading to Cloutsham and over to another road, which heads up over Dunkery Hill. Here, turn right and walk up until you see a wooden sign on the left marked 'Public bridleway Dunster Path, Brockwell'.

Take this path. At the next wooden sign, continue towards Wootton Courtenay. You'll be treated to fine views of, among others, North Hill and Wootton Common, all along the Dunster Path.

At the next sign, ignore the left-hand turning to Brockwell and walk straight on for 'Dunster Path, Ford and Spangate'. Approximately 55 m (60 yards) after this sign, look for a small inconspicuous path on the right. Take this route. On reaching a junction, turn right and join the Macmillan Way West, which

The Macmillan Way West with Wootton Courtenay in the distance

climbs up to a road and continues on the other side all the way and beyond our primary objective: Dunkery Beacon.

There are fine expansive views both sides now, and if you're lucky you might catch a glimpse of a herd of deer gracefully moving across the landscape. It's a prime location for spotting them.

Close to the road, you'll reach a small cairn marking a crossroads of paths. Go straight ahead until you meet the road. Cross over and continue on the wide path, marked 'Dunkery Beacon ¾'. The beacon will be in view as you tread towards it, climbing all the time.

Soon, you'll reach the beacon, having stopped to watch – if you're lucky – the sturdy Exmoor ponies present on this part of the moor. The commanding stone hive-shaped beacon was built in September 1935 to celebrate the handing over of Dunkery Hill to the National Trust by Sir Thomas Acland, Colonel Wiggin and Allan Hughes.

Being the highest point on Exmoor, it's a windy spot but on a calm day or using the beacon as shelter from an enthusiastic wind, this is the point to dig out the sandwiches and flask from your rucksack – partly because you can see for miles.

When ready to continue your walk, looking northwards, head down the wide grass path on the other side of the beacon from

Dunkery Beacon

which you approached. Ignore a path on your right and continue your descent with vistas of Porlock Hill, the Bristol Channel and Bossington Hill ahead.

When you reach a path crossroads near the bottom of the descent, turn right on to Dicky's Path. The path travels into the throat of Aller Combe, crosses water and then emerges from the combe. Soon, you'll be looking towards Webber's Post and the car park, with the unmistakable white church of Selworthy in the background.

Ignore a path crossing your route, next to a tree, and carry on around Hollow Combe. Upon reaching a split, take the left-hand path. Continue straight on, even when a wide path cuts across you on two occasions. Soon you'll meet a tarmaced road. Cross and continue back to your car.

DID YOU KNOW?

- The shortest route to the beacon is from Dunkery Gate, just as the road comes off Dunkery Hill and winds its way down to the B3224. The distance of this route is around 1.2 km (¾ mile).
- There are several Bronze Age burial mounds in the vicinity of Dunkery Beacon, some you'll pass on Walk 7.

This walk encompasses, among other features, open moorland, deep valleys, winding streams, ancient cairns and wildlife – and the serenity one comes to expect from this beautiful part of the world.

If undertaking the walk early morning or during the evening, in particular, there is a good chance you'll see herds of deer scattered across the moorland: at least fifty deer were spotted when I last covered the route, which begins with a climb to Dunkery Beacon, the highest point on Exmoor.

The lack of recognised car parks means fewer people are seen treading the paths west of the beacon. That is a bonus as you stride along the ridge to two distinctive Bronze Age barrows: Little Rowbarrow and Great Rowbarrow, which, in fact, are part of a string of capped summits along Exmoor's central ridge.

The path descends, crosses Wilmersham Common and heads northwards before turning south-westerly and running above Nutscale Reservoir, the most secluded of Exmoor's reservoirs,

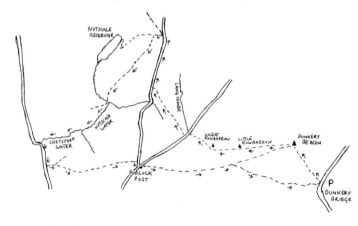

tucked away in a quiet valley with no public access. Built in 1942, it supplies water to Porlock and Minehead. When full, it's just over 12 m (40 feet) deep and contains around 178 million litres of water.

The path drops to Nutscale Water and for just under a mile runs beside this and Chetsford Water in a deep valley across Open Access land with no recognised path.

The return leg of the walk is equally impressive and largely level-walking.

Distance: 13.25 km/8¼ miles approx. | Time: 3½ hours approx. | Parking and starting point: Car park at Dunkery Bridge, below the beacon (grid ref: SS 895 406). There is a £1 voluntary car park donation. Look for the National Trust collection box on the other side of the road | Toilets at start: None | Difficulties: Plenty of level walking with just a few climbs, the steepest sections being up to the beacon and a short stretch of road from the bridge at Chetsford Water until you turn off on to the moorside | Map: Explorer map OL9

THE WALK

From the car park, bear right on to the road and walk approximately 68 m (70 yards) before turning left on to a public bridleway to Dunkery Beacon. It's a straightforward climb to the beacon, just over ¾ km (½ mile) away. But if you stop to catch your breath, be sure to turn around and admire the beautiful countryside which rolls out in front of you.

Eventually reaching a toposcope, on your right at the summit, take the second path on the left, tracking westwards from the beacon along a ridge. After around 500 m, (546 yards) ignore a track crossing your path, marked by a small cairn on the right. Continue straight on.

Soon, you'll pass – on your right – the ancient cairns of Little Rowbarrow and, as the path bends right, Great Rowbarrow.

LEFT *Deer roam the hillside near Dunkery* BELOW *Heading away from Great Rowbarrow near Dunkery Beacon with Wilmersham Common in the distance*

Both date from the Bronze Age and are around 3,500–4,000 years old.

Just after passing a small fenced-off area on your right, the path widens and drops. Reaching a road, turn left and after about 18 m (20 yards) join a narrow path on the right at Lang Combe Head. It's unsigned and not the easiest to locate, but it's to the left of a spring and small tree.

You'll pass Lang Combe on the right with fine views across to Bossington Hill in the distance. Ignore a path running across your route. Soon you'll catch sight of a road ahead, just as the path splits off to the right. Carry on up over and join the road. Turn right and walk along. It's not the busiest of roads but keep your eyes and ears open for approaching cars; chances are, the drivers will be admiring the sweeping views, just like you.

Continue until a large lay-by on the left. Turn left on to a track at the end of the lay-by, just before a tree and post marking a public bridleway to Lucott, one mile away.

Our route, down a tarmaced track, leads to Nutscale Reservoir (no public admittance), but turns left not far along the track on to a stony, rutted path, running above Nutscale. Sadly, most of the reservoir is obscured from view, save brief glimpses as we walk along.

Eventually, the path begins to drop – with Great Hill to the right – down to Nutscale Water. Ignore a path joining on the right.

Reaching the water, cross using the conveniently positioned stones. Don't take the path climbing steeply on the right; instead, retain the water close on the left and make your way between the trees. In various places, there is no obvious path so it's a case of picking your way.

Soon you'll have to cross the water again, just as a narrow sheep track climbs up on the right. Almost immediately, you'll need to cross back again, as the stream splits with Embercombe Water to the left. Carry on ahead, now following Chetsford Water, which will remain on the left all the way.

Nutscale Reservoir, seen from a track just below our route

After a while, you'll see a small road bridge ahead. Aim for it across land which is usually muddy and boggy.

At the road, turn left, cross the bridge – under which Chetsford Water flows – and follow the road around the sharp bend and up the steep incline. Be careful because it's a busier road than we've encountered so far on this walk.

On seeing a wide path crossing the road, turn left on to it. The entrance is marked by stones preventing vehicular use. Ignore a track on the left going down into Ember Combe and continue cutting across the side of the moor. At a tarmaced road, don't cross on to the small path ahead, turn right and walk along until you reach a junction, at a signpost named Porlock Post. Cross the road to join a track marked by a post left of a metal gate, indicating a public bridleway to Dunkery Beacon, 2½ miles away. You're joining the Macmillan Way West and will stay on it for around 2 km (1¼ miles).

Ignore any paths joining on the left as you walk along

Nutscale Water running towards Nutscale Reservoir

the stony track, close to a treed boundary, which occasionally through gaps offers walkers a glimpse of the green, pastoral landscape beyond.

Reaching a split with Dunkery Beacon to your left, take the right-hand option, again retaining the treed border on the right. Follow the path down to the road and your car at Dunkery Bridge.

DID YOU KNOW?

- It's estimated that Exmoor is home to around 3,000 red deer.
- Chetsford Water helps to feed Horner Water, which escapes into the sea at Bossington Bay. The length from source to mouth is about 8 miles.

This walk begins in the south-western corner of Dunster, a fine medieval village just 3 km (2 miles) from Minehead. During holiday periods it's packed, being one of Exmoor's most visited spots.

While the constant flow of vehicles making its way through the village's traffic light system can be tiresome, it doesn't spoil the experience of strolling along the cobbled pavements, marvelling at all the listed buildings and enjoying the many attractions, such as the elegant National Trust-owned castle. From its lofty position above the village, it has tourists reaching for their cameras. A castle has existed here since Norman times, although today's building received a makeover in the late nineteenth century.

I suggest exploring the village at the end of the walk, once the hard work is out of the way. The route leaves Dunster via its famous packhorse bridge, crossing the River Avill, and enters Dunster Woodland, part of the 9,900-acre Crown Estate-owned Dunster Estate extending from the ancient harbour town of Watchet to Minehead.

We follow a well marked route taking us up on to Gallox Hill and along to Bat's Castle, where you'll see the remains of an Iron Age hill fort and settlement built in the sixth century BC. Whichever way you turn, you'll be feasting your eyes on stunning views of woodland, moorland, pastureland and the West Somerset coast.

The path drops off the hill and heads across fields, just before reaching Carhampton, a village 3 miles south-east of Minehead. We return to Dunster across the Deer Park, built by the Luttrell Family who lived in the castle for over 600 years; its construction was not only to complement the area's outstanding beauty but for practical reasons, too: generating a reliable supply of venison for the castle.

Once back at your car, relax and remove your walking boots before enjoying a cream tea or spot of lunch in the pretty village of Dunster.

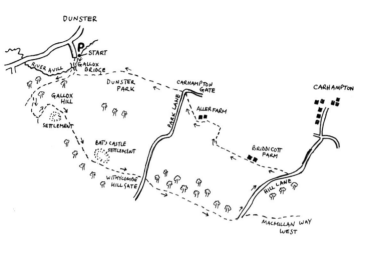

*Distance: 7.25 km/4½ miles approx. | Time: 2 hours approx. |
Parking and starting point: Small pay-and-display car park in Park
Street (grid ref: SS 989 432) | Toilets at start: None | Difficulties: No
particular difficulties, although there is a gradual climb up through
the woods to Gallox Hill | Map: Explorer map OL9*

THE WALK

From the car park, turn left and cross Gallox Bridge, a packhorse
bridge we cross twice during this walk. It played a key role in
Dunster's wool trade during medieval times. Spanning the River
Avill (you'll also see it spelt 'Aville' and 'Avil'), it enabled traders
to cross the water with their pack animals; it's one of the village's
highlights and a protected Grade I listed building.

Follow in the direction of the wooden sign marked 'Dunster
Forest', passing a row of thatched cottages. On meeting a junction
of paths, follow the middle track leading into Dunster Woodland,

An information board at Bat's Castle

signed 'Bat's Castle (Crown Estate Land)'.

The path climbs steadily through the forest, which is managed carefully to not only supply high quality timber but to enhance the treasured wildlife discovered in this corner of Exmoor. Eventually, the path splits, at which point you'll need to swing left, marked 'Bat's Castle ¾ mile away'.

The path continues its ascent and at the next wooden sign, turn left for Bat's Castle. As you leave the trees behind, the grassy path begins to level off before twisting and dropping to a further sign. Carry on ahead for Bat's Castle with the path climbing again.

As you approach the summit, which reaches nearly 213 m (700 feet), the wide grass path splits. Continue ahead, ignoring the route veering left. Once past the wooden barrier, you reach the castle – or what remains of the sixth-century BC Iron Age hill fort. The huge ditch and bank are all that have survived, sadly, of this circular enclosure, but it's still an impressive site and boasts a wonderful vantage point with panoramic views, including across the Bristol Channel to South Wales, down to Dunster and over towards Dunkery Beacon.

Near Bat's Castle looking north-east towards Wootton Courtenay

Looking back towards Dunster from Bat's Castle area

Continuing on your way along this well-marked route, the path narrows and passes through another wooden barrier down to a sign. Carry on ahead, marked 'Deer Park Circuit'. Reaching the next waymark, at the entrance to dense woodland, ignore paths on your left and right and carry straight on through the trees.

At a five-bar gate, go through and you'll see a wooden bench ahead of you. Turn right and immediately left, signed 'Bridleway Withycombe Hill ½'. Ignore the track on the left and go straight on. Don't be distracted by other paths. Soon you'll reach another wooden five-bar gate. After entering, trees will only be fringing the left-hand side of the path as you run along Withycombe Hill, affording you the chance to enjoy the scenery, looking across to Black Hill and back towards wooded Croydon Hill.

Carhampton from Hill Lane

Straight on at the next sign, marked 'Public path 1¼ Carhampton'. As the path twists left, still edging trees, you'll notice another wooden sign. Bend around to the left, following '1¼ Carhampton'. The track, known as Hill Lane, drops and continues through a five-bar gate. It's a badly rutted and very stony surface so watch your ankles.

Soon, you'll catch sight of the village of Carhampton, with the Bristol Channel in the distance. As the path leaves the trees behind, your route is now bordered by fields. At a wooden sign, turn left, following the public footpath for 'Dunster 2 via Aller Farm'.

The path takes you through Briddicott Farm and beyond. As it's used by farm vehicles, the surface can become very muddy and slippery during inclement weather.

Continue through two metal gates and on reaching the next, go through, heading in the direction of the arrow, taking you diagonally across a field to another metal gate and a yellow-capped post. Go through and keep left, close to the hedge.

At another metal gate, on the left, where you'll see more yellow waymarks, enter the field, keeping right of the hedge, with Aller Farm ahead. Go through a metal gate, turning immediately left, directed by another wooden arrowed sign. The track skirts Aller Farm, splitting opposite a metal gate. Carry on, between two hay barns.

The track enters a field, marked by yellow paint on a gate post; the gate itself has been removed. Turn right and trek across the field to an old stile. Climb over and at a wooden signpost, go through a metal gate. This location is known as Carhampton Gate, one of the official entrances into the medieval deer park; others include Withycombe Hill Gate. Before the A39 route was constructed, this was the main route into Dunster from this direction.

Continue on the public footpath to Dunster, a mile away. Head down over the field, keeping tight to the field boundary on your right, with the resplendent Dunster Castle ahead. Through a wooden gate, next to a metal one, and carry on.

Soon the outskirts of Dunster village appear and the route swings around to the thatched cottages and car park where you left the car. After a kissing gate, turn right and go back over Gallox Bridge to the car park on the right.

Alternatively, and highly recommended, make sure you've got time left on your parking ticket and wander around Dunster. The village's many offerings include the seventeenth-century octagonal-shaped yarn market where centuries ago trading in the region's cloth industry thrived. Tucked away, close to the village church, is the tranquil Memorial Garden where you can sit and reflect on the walk you've just completed, while the run of quaint shops, cafés and, of course, Dunster Castle means there is much to admire about this medieval village.

DID YOU KNOW?

- The Crown Estate owns and manages Dunster Estate, which incorporates Dunster Forest. Within the forest you'll find well-organised and clearly marked trails exploring the likes of Dunster's deer park, the forest and, of course, Bat's Castle.
- Next time you visit this part of Exmoor, opt for the Tall Trees Trail: this impressive grove, dating back to the 1870s, contains an array of exotic and high-reaching specimens, including a 60-m (197-foot) Douglas fir, classed as England's tallest tree.

Grabbist – Dunster – Minehead

Like any area of outstanding natural beauty, and Exmoor is certainly that, there are walks which are popular with seemingly everybody in the district and those less trodden. This scintillating ridge walk – which I call Grabbist, although Grabbist Hill itself occupies only part of the landscape – is rarely crowded; in fact, every time I stroll along its top, head swishing everywhere while soaking up the glorious panoramic views, I'm usually alone, save for the birds singing their hearts out and the breeze tickling the trees.

This steep-sided hill – which towards Dunster has been christened the 'Giant's Chair', due to its shape – is an underestimated corner of Exmoor, ignored or unconsidered by many holidaymakers and walkers who choose Dunkery, Horner, Porlock Hill and other popular spots, blissfully unaware of what they're missing.

And what they're missing is a fine walk which begins on the south-western edge of Minehead and heads into the deeply wooded Periton Combe before climbing steeply around Periton Hill on to the ridge.

Views on top are striking: to your left, you look seawards across the Bristol Channel to the Welsh coast, ahead up the channel towards Weston-super-Mare and right along the Avill Valley towards Dunkery .

Turning easterly, we follow the Macmillan Way West, a branch path off the main long-distance Macmillan Way (see 'Introduction' for details of this long-distance route), until dropping down into Dunster, a beautifully preserved medieval village we skirt before heading north to the coast. Among the points of interest you'll see as you edge the village is a dovecote, believed to have been part of the monastic estate of the Benedictine Priory of Dunster.

Over 7.5 m (25 feet) tall, it's a fine example of a medieval circular-towered dovecote.

On reaching the coastline beyond Dunster Railway Station, we turn left and walk back to Minehead along the edge of the golf links. After a pleasant walk along the sea front and up through the town's main street, it's back to the parking place.

Distance: 13 km/8 miles approx. | Time: 3½ hours approx. | Parking and starting point: Roadside parking at the top of Parkhouse Road, Minehead (grid ref: SS 957 456) | Toilets at start: None | Difficulties: There is plenty of level walking on this route but the climb to the top of Grabbist is very steep. The descent to Dunster is short but steep at times, too | Map: Explorer map OL9

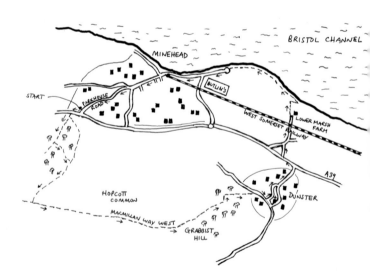

THE WALK

Leave your car at the top of Parkhouse Road (a residential street) and turn right at the junction. Walk around 180 m (200 yards) to a track on your left, signed 'Public bridleway Wootton Courtenay'. Take care walking along this precarious stretch of road because there are no pavements and cars rush along.

The stony track passes an electricity sub-station on the right, while a brook on your left switches sides occasionally. Go around the red metal barrier and past the wooden sign indicating you're entering Crown Estate land. You're now in Periton Combe, part of the larger Dunster Woodland.

Continue for about 460 m (500 yards), ignoring smaller paths on both sides, until reaching the first main split. Take the left-hand route, crossing the brook, which usually flows unless we're experiencing a drought, and head up through the trees. Ignore a grass track, around 18 m (20 yards) on the right, and continue until paths form a T-junction.

Turn right and begin the steepest part of the walk, signed 'Bridleway Wootton Courtenay 1½'. As you begin emerging from underneath the tree canopy, you'll reach another junction of paths. Bear left by a wooden blue-capped post; to your relief, you've just about reached the end of the ascent.

At the next blue-capped post, positioned alongside a further junction, turn left. Now on the ridge of the hill, it's downhill or flat walking all the way from this point, bar a short climb back to your car at the end of the walk.

You're now treading along the Macmillan Way West. The path runs left of a dense area of trees, by which time you've already been treated to some fine views of North Hill – but better is yet to come. Ignoring any paths on either side, continue ahead along the top of the hill.

On a clear day, you can see for miles up the coast with the small islands of Steep Holm and Flat Holm, in the Bristol Channel, clearly visible. To your left, you have Minehead and the sea; on

A lone dog walker on top Grabbist Hill

your right, the glorious Exmoor countryside.

You'll reach two wooden barriers at a junction of paths. The signpost shows you need to carry on, signed 'Public bridleway Dunster 2'. Again, there is a dense stretch of trees immediately right; ignore the right-hand path entering the woods.

Pass a wooden bench on the right and at the next signpost, close to another seat, follow the direction of 'Bridleway Grabbist Hill 1'. At the next fork, keep right.

When the path splits three ways, veer left. As your route descends, head straight on at the next wooden sign marked, 'Bridleway', with a wooden bench and metal 'National Trust Grabbist Hill' sign on the right.

The path runs to the right of a field boundary. At the next sign, turn left for Dunster, half a mile away. The path drops steadily to another wooden sign. Ignore the right-hand route, following '½ Dunster via Conduit Lane' instead.

The path drops quickly now as you enter a wooded area but soon bends left to a large wooden gate. Go through, following the sign for 'Bridleway Dunster ¼'.

Walking on top Grabbist Hill before dropping down to Dunster

You're now in Conduit Lane, and as the name suggests it can be wet and muddy, so make sure your walking boots don't leak! When the lane finally joins the road, ignore Hangers Way on your immediate right, turning right instead on to the road with a small water channel on your right-hand side.

You're on the outskirts of Dunster now and after passing thatched cottages on the right, turn first left into Priory Green, with the Church of St George on your right.

Walk under the stone archway and follow the road. But take care because there are sharp bends, no pavements and it's narrow in places.

You'll pass the peaceful Church of St George's Memorial Garden on your right while left is a medieval circular-towered dovecote: both are worth exploring before continuing along the road, under another stone archway on a sharp bend.

The road turns to the right and soon joins the main road out of Dunster village. At the junction, turn left and cross as soon as possible to pick up the pavement.

Pass Dunster Visitor Centre on the right, a row of shops and a car park before approaching a major traffic light system at a main A39 junction. Just before, cross over and walk under the subway, marked by a blue sign. Emerging from the subway, turn left for Minehead. Keep left of the metal railings when the path splits and turns right at Laundry Cottage.

Walk down the road until you reach a junction with farm buildings in front. Turn right, signed 'Dunster Station/Dunster Beach'. Walk over the road bridge and carry on for Dunster Station, ignoring a right-hand turning.

At the station, walk over the railway crossing – taking care because there are no automatic gates. The road bends left and passes the entrance to Lower Marsh Farm on your right. Here, you'll pick up a public footpath sign.

Passing the Old Manor, you'll reach a metal gate. The track now narrows and runs alongside farm buildings before passing through another two metal gates. You'll soon have open fields either side.

Walking along The Warren towards Minehead with Dunster Beach in the background

At the end of the track, turn right, through a metal gate on to land owned by the Minehead and West Somerset Golf Club. This is the point where golfers reach the halfway mark on this splendid 18-hole golf links, running along the coast from Minehead to Dunster Beach. Golfers will be heading back towards the golf house from here, so keep your ears open for cries of 'Fore!'.

The path travels over a wooden footbridge before reaching a wooden sign with the remains of a pebble-built war hut on the seashore. Follow signs for Minehead, staying close to the pebbles. Avoid straying on to the fairways as you wander along, with the beautiful hump-shaped North Hill ahead and the large white canopy of Butlin's holiday camp.

The path edges the pebbles all the way and fine views abound. As you approach the golf clubhouse on your left, keep right of a fence, following the footpath along the pebble bank.

The path becomes sandy and drops into a small car park leading out on to a mini-roundabout. Turn right, keeping on the

Walking back to Minehead along The Warren

pavement, and climb the concrete steps on to the promenade.

Walk along the sea front, passing entrances to Butlin's and amusement arcades on your left. Eventually, you'll reach a train station, home of the West Somerset Railway. It's the longest standard gauge steam railway in Britain, running 32 km (20 miles) through outstanding countryside from Minehead to Bishops Lydeard, just outside Taunton.

Carry on up The Avenue, Minehead's main shopping street, ignoring any roads on either side, until you arrive at a main junction, called Floyds Corner. The Queen Anne statue, a landmark of the town, stands at the back of Wellington Square, to your left. The statue, by sculptor Francis Bird, was presented to the town in 1791 and has stood in its current location since 1893.

Walk on, passing another rank of shops on either side. The road bends right and when safe to do so, cross (take care because it's a busy road). Join Parkhouse Road. Continue on this street, ignoring turnings on either side. When the road becomes steep and you pass a post box on your right, it's only a few more yards (uphill, unfortunately) to your car.

DID YOU KNOW?

- Between April and May, skylarks nest near the footpath running alongside the golf links, so listen out for birdsong and make sure you tread carefully.
- The course at the Minehead and West Somerset Golf Club is the second oldest in the South West.

WALK 10:   *North Hill*

Growing up in Minehead, on the edge of the National Park, meant North Hill was right on my doorstep and, therefore, the hill I explored most; for me, it's one of the best areas of Exmoor and this route offers walkers the chance to experience the hill in all its glory, taking them from one end to the other and back again.

When striding atop the hill, you have the Bristol Channel on one side, the unfolding Exmoor landscape on the other – the perfect combination.

Along the route there are myriad seats, ideal spots for picnics, endless photo opportunites, countless paths heading in every direction and ample birdlife and wildlife, including deer and the wonderfully robust Exmoor ponies.

The 5-mile ridge stretches from Minehead in the east to Bossington in the west; this walk follows stretches of the South West Coast Path, a National Trail, returning along the Rugged Alternative Coast Path winding its way around the hilly contours – in part being East Combe and Henners Combe – back to Minehead.

Among the walk's many interesting features are the ruins of Burgundy Chapel, although, sadly, they're largely hidden by undergrowth nowadays. Not much is known about this medieval chapel, including its origins, although it has been suggested that the Luttrells – a well-known local family who bought Dunster Castle in the fourteenth century and lived there some 600 years before handing it over to the National Trust – were behind its construction in gratitude for a safe return from the fifteenth-century Burgundian Wars.

This mortared stone structure which comprises, it seems, of a chapel and domestic dwelling was built of local sandstone and record of it appears in the Luttrell household accounts in the

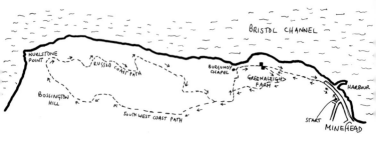

early 1400s as Bircombe Chapel. Over the years, it became largely hidden by trees and weeds until excavations in 1940 revealed the remains once more.

Distance: 17.75 km/11 miles approx. | Time: 4½ hours approx. | Parking and starting point: Free roadside parking in Blenheim Road, Minehead (grid ref: SS 971 466) | Toilets at start: None, but toilets on the left, just past the Old Ship Aground pub | Difficulties: A long walk, steep in many places, particularly the descent to Burgundy Chapel. But there is a lot of level walking, too, particularly the first half of the walk | Map: Explorer map OL9

THE WALK

Leaving your car in Blenheim Road, walk towards the sea front. At the junction, opposite the sea wall, turn left and stroll along, passing The Quay Inn on your left, Minehead harbour and The Old Ship Aground, another pub, on your right.

Continue to a small roundabout, keeping left and joining a public bridleway, signed 'Greenaleigh Farm'. The path climbs through woods with various tracks joining from the left – ignore them all.

At a wooden sign, follow towards 'Bridleway Greenaleigh Farm ⅓'. The path joins a semi-tarmaced lane and now you'll pick up 'Coast Path' signs. Walk straight ahead, ignoring a right-hand track descending to fields fringing the seashore.

Pass the National Trust sign for Greenaleigh Point but just before the farm, bend sharp left at a sign for 'Coast Path Porlock'. The path turns back on itself and climbs through the woods. Continue on this route, turning left and through a wooden five-bar gate. The farm once belonged to the Dunster Castle Estate and was an important dairy farm in the area, supplying milk to Minehead.

At a junction by a wooden gate and bench, turn right for 'Bridleway North Hill'. The bridleway emerges from under the treed canopy. Down below, you'll be leaving Greenaleigh Farm behind and greeted by head-turning views of the Bristol Channel and the rocky coastline.

At the next sign, again marked 'Bridleway North Hill', turn left. The route ascends to another wooden sign where you need to go right for 'Coast Path Bossington 4'. It's straight ahead at the next bridleway sign, carrying the acorn symbol used on National Trails.

You're now following the South West Coast Path. Ignore any paths appearing on your left and continue ahead, through a wooden gate and past the National Trust sign informing you that you're entering Holnicote Estate land.

The path edges a field for some time. Go through another wooden gate and don't deviate from this path. Cross a small tarmaced road and follow signs for 'Bossington/Porlock'. Enjoy the channel views as you stroll along.

At the next signpost, turn right. Continue following the acorn signs but when a broad path joins from the left with views of Porlock Bay greeting you, keep right.

At a split, stay right, following the Coast Path sign, heading in the direction of the sea. The path begins to sweep around, with a cairn atop Bossington Hill to your left, before descending and splitting. Keep right, joining the route signed 'Rugged Alternative Coast Path Minehead'.

Looking down across Porlock Bay from near Bossington Hill

You're now turning back for the return leg of the walk. Ignore any paths on the left. This route is less frequented and you may not pass another walker as you return to Minehead.

The path weaves in and out of several valleys and combes punctuating this stretch of the coast. When it splits, either route is fine because they soon join up. At the next junction, head down the left-hand path signed 'Rugged Path Only, 3 miles'. Reaching a gate, go through and the path will climb and drop regularly, often running alongside a field boundary. You'll cross a handful of streams but remain on the main path as it twists its way in and out of the deep valleys.

Pass through another wooden gate. Then, later, the path drops steeply to two further streams. Once across, ignore the small, hardly discernible path on your right and continue up the hill.

Reaching the top, turn left at a wooden post, at the head of a gully, turning right at the next post and climbing once more. Go over a stile, next to a five-bar gate, and follow the grass track, veering right.

When a path joins from the left, bend right and walk past a

ABOVE, BELOW AND OVERLEAF *The rugged coastpath on North Hill*

Minehead harbour

wooden bench before turning left. At the next junction, go left on to a marked bridleway.

You're now on familiar ground briefly, having covered this part of the path on the outward leg. At the signpost, turn left, downhill, for 'Coastpath Minehead Harbour'. Straight ahead at the next junction, for 'Permitted Footpath Burgundy Chapel'. This path is extremely steep and care must be taken, particularly when the surface is wet.

When you see a wooden bench at a junction, turn right. The steep descent continues. Finally reaching the bottom, a small stony path on the left takes you to what remains of the chapel; sadly, when I last completed the walk, flourishing undergrowth obscured my view.

To continue the walk, you need to follow the path on the right which will pass a sign marked 'Greenaleigh Point'. After a small wooden gate, the fields of the farm soon appear, down on your left.

Reaching a split, with the farmhouse in view, keep left to a five-bar gate. Once through, you have a choice: detour around the farmhouse by following the 'Footpath Greenaleigh Beach' sign, walking along the pebbles before re-joining the main path further along or, like me, remain on the main path through the farm and on to a semi-tarmaced track.

Continue straight on, signed 'Coast Path Minehead 1', again on ground covered on your outward journey. When the track bends right and rises, take the coast path on the left.

At the next wooden sign, pick the left fork for Minehead, three quarters of a miles away, which drops through trees to a tarmac path and open green, known as Culvercliffe Walk.

With the sea to your left, walk until reaching the familiar roundabout. Retrace your steps past the Old Ship Aground pub, the harbour and The Quay Inn to Blenheim Road, and your car, on the right.

DID YOU KNOW?

- The *Balmoral*, a classic cruise ship, and the *Waverley*, reputedly the last sea-going paddle steamer in the world, run a regular programme of visits to Minehead harbour during the summer period.
- Remains of a Second World War tank training ground and radar station can be found on North Hill.
- Minehead is referred to as the Gateway to Exmoor.

Quiet Woodcombe, on the western edge of Minehead, is the starting point for this walk. Once a separate entity, urban growth has seen the two merge.

This is a peaceful walk and for much of the time you're unlikely to pass another soul. Its relatively short duration makes it ideal if you only have a morning or afternoon free – or perhaps fancy a short early evening summer walk.

It's an interesting route, taking you towards the tiny hamlet of Bratton before heading up the slopes of North Hill via woodland and fields. Your stay on top is brief but you'll enjoy a fair share of stunning views before dropping back down to Woodcombe, where the walk began.

Distance: 5.25 km/3¼ miles approx. | Time: 1 hour 45 mins approx. | Parking and starting point: Roadside parking in Bratton Lane, just as the houses end (grid ref: SS 953 456) | Toilets at start: None | Difficulties: The route is steep in places, especially after Wydon Farm. The beginning of the descent into Woodcombe requires care, especially if wet under foot | Map: Explorer map OL9

THE WALK

On leaving your car, follow the road which soon turns into a tarmaced lane. The lane descends and you'll pass a sign on the right for Woodcombe Lodge before meeting a junction.

Head in the direction of Hindon and Wydon Farms, which are signposted, before turning right upon reaching the 'No Through Road' sign, near Bratton Court Farm.

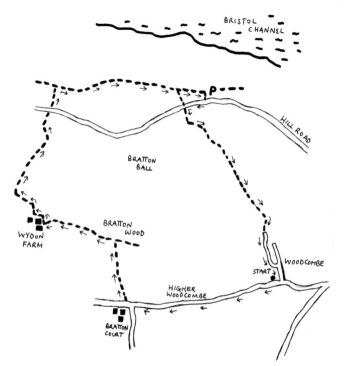

Follow the sign for 'Public Footpath Woodcombe'. The path cuts between two fields and rises to a five-bar gate. Go through and keep left, now turning away from Woodcombe.

Pass through another wooden gate and keep left. Follow the path running alongside the fence with holly trees on your left, beyond which you'll enjoy glimpses of the beautiful rural landscape stretching out towards Dunkery Hill.

The path begins to drop, finally reaching Wydon Farm. Look for the sign stating 'Footpath avoiding farmyard', slightly obscured by a wooden handrail.

Skirting the farm, climb a stile into another field and follow the sign directing you around the farmyard. Climb a further stile, staying close to the field's border. The path bends left and soon

Heading up on to the side of North Hill from Bratton Court

reaches a five-bar gate. Enter the adjoining field where views back towards Minehead, Conygar Tower on the outskirts of Dunster, Blue Anchor and the Somerset coastline are stunning.

Look out for a bridleway sign. The track sweeps around and becomes deep-rutted as it takes you above Wydon Farm. The gradient increases in this section, the steepest of the entire walk, save a stretch of path dropping into Woodcombe.

As the track bends sharply right, while remaining close to a fence, follow the 'Bridleway North Hill' sign. You'll need a moment to get your breath back, so turn around and admire the view of Dunkery Beacon and surrounding countryside.

When the track meets a five-bar gate, go through and turn immediately left. Around 55 m (60 yards) on and you'll reach North Hill Road. Cross and walk ahead until meeting a crossroads of paths. Head down to the field boundary, turning right on to the

TOP *Skirting Wydon Farm en route to the top of North Hill*
ABOVE *On top North Hill with Bristol Channel on the left*

South West Coast Path (see 'Introduction' for details of this long-distance walk), with views of the Bristol Channel and the Welsh coast beyond.

Through a wooden gate – indicating that you're leaving Holnicote Estate, a 5,026-hectare National Trust-managed estate – and keep right of the acorn-emblazoned sign.

At the next sign, carry on, marked 'Bridleway', until reaching a crossroads. Head in the direction of the 'Woodcombe Bratton' sign, veering right and reaching a car park. Walk out on to the North Hill road. Turn right and look for a path on the left, around 119 m (130 yards) up the road, signed, 'Public bridleway Woodcombe 1'.

The path is extremely steep as it winds down into the valley. Ignore a sign indicating Bratton to the right, continuing straight on, marked 'Public bridleway Woodcombe 1'. Ignore a path, too, appearing on your left.

Soon the path follows a small stream. At a gate, go through and look for another gate, on the left, marked 'Squire Field'. At this point, the path turns into a muddy track and then a tarmaced lane. With the brook on your left, walk down the lane – soon houses will edge both sides. The lane bends left before reaching a junction, named 'Higher Orchard'. Turn right. At the next junction, you'll be back on the road where you left your car.

DID YOU KNOW?

- Bratton Court, in the hamlet of Bratton, is a Grade I listed building and was originally used as a manor house. The open hall dates back to the fourteenth century. Now, it serves as a farmhouse.

Everyone loves a mystery and this walk contains one in the shape of Clicket, a long-forgotten and, in many respects, mysterious remains of a crumbling village, hidden amongst trees and bushes in one of the quiet valleys explored on this route.

Little is known about Clicket, except that the settlement contained houses, footbridges, a mill servicing local farms, a lime kiln and was abandoned during the nineteenth century. In fact, many people don't even know that this tiny rural community existed. But five families were recorded as residents here in the 1880s, although fast-forward a decade and they had disappeared.

The eerie surroundings of this dead village are experienced during the first half of this walk, which begins in the sedate village of Timberscombe, situated in a valley aside the main A396, nearly three miles from the medieval village of Dunster.

The walk takes you south of Timberscombe along quiet valleys and lanes which are less visited than other areas of Exmoor. On the final stages, prior to reaching the A396 just minutes from your car, you'll pass through Bickham Farm, a point of interest in that Bickham Manor was recorded in the Domesday survey.

Distance: 13 km/8 miles approx. | Time: 3¼ hours approx. | Parking and starting point: Roadside parking in Brewers Green, just off the main A396 (grid ref: SS 955 421) | Toilets at start: None | Difficulties: There are gradual rises in places but overall it's a comfortable route to walk | Map: Explorer map OL9

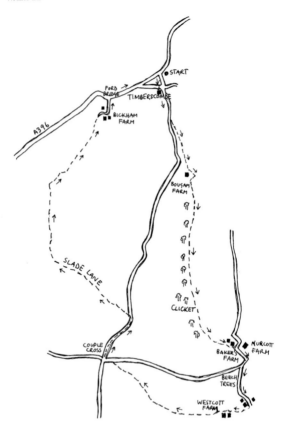

THE WALK

After leaving your car in Brewers Green, just off the main road, join Vicarage Court. Turn left after The Lion Inn, climbing steps into the grounds of St Petrock Church, opposite the pub.

Walk around the back of the church and on to a road. Head up the road, which has a slight gradient, passing Church View Farm. After around 360 m (400 yards), you'll notice a track on the left, marked 'Luxborough via Clicket'.

Follow it until reaching a 'No Right of Way' sign. Here, climb the stile on the right. The path skirts the field. Veer right before the gate, following the yellow-marked posts. Edge the field, keeping right at the fork, signposted 'Clicket 1 Mile'. Over a stile and follow the path which continues to skirt fields while a stream meanders below on your left.

Go through a gate. Carry on along the edge of the forest to another gate. Follow the path signed 'Beech Tree Cross', although the actual inscription is 'Beach Tree Cross'.

At a track junction, turn left and follow the path, keeping your eyes open for a turning on the right, with a yellow marked post. The path weaves its way through woods and a gate into a field. Cross the field and climb the stile before continuing towards Clicket. Look out for sculpted models of wild boars in the woods on the right – quite a novelty.

At the confluence of two rivers, keep left and mount the flank

A peaceful valley just outside Timberscombe

of a spur, keeping the river, below, to your left. On the right, you'll soon spot what remains of Clicket, partially obscured by undergrowth. Sadly, it's little more than dilapidated stone walls of long-forgotten buildings. Continue on your way, passing through a gate, crossing a field and over a stile.

You'll pass redundant quarry buildings on your right, amongst hazelnut and ash trees, with lush green fields on your left. Eventually, the path reaches Bakers Farm and joins a road. Turn right, walking up the road for around 500 m (⅓ mile) before bending right with Nurcott Farm on your left.

Pass Lower Ley Farm on the left. Ignore the public bridleway sign, stating 'Timberscombe 3½'. Bend right and at '3 Beach Trees' (this must be a spelling mistake, the correct version being 'Beech') crossroads, turn left for 'Luxborough ¼, Roadwater 4½'.

Enjoy the views across the Brendons as the high-banked road twists and turns, passing Westcott Farm on your right. Just after the road sign for West View, turn right on to a public footpath marked 'Over Stowey 1 mile'.

Go over a stile, through a gate, across a field, through another gate and across the road leading to Westcott Farm. Once on the other side of the road, go through another gate into a field. Skirt the field and go through a five-bar gate before climbing a stile immediately on your left. Turn right and walk around the edge of a further field.

Over another stile at the end of the field, then another. Edge the next field. You'll pass Throat Cottage, an isolated pink dwelling on your left. The path here is barely discernible but eventually joins a track. Enter through a metal gate. Keep right of the stream, crossing another field and through a further metal gate.

Across three more fields, via stiles, then continue along the edge of a fence by a large pink house. Go through a wooden five-bar gate, turning right on to a track, signed 'Public footpath – County Road ½'.

Beech Tree junction near Churchtown

At the top of the track, marking the entrance to a property named Old Stowey, take a left on to a road. At the next junction, turn right for 'Timberscombe 3'.

Soak up the views on your left of Dunkery Beacon and along to the woods of Grabbist before passing, also on your left, the entrance to Stowey Farm. Continue along the road, flanked by beech trees, passing Allercott Farm on the right.

Turn left and go through a gate, following the sign marked 'Restricted Byway – Pitt Bridge 1½'. Enter Slade Lane, canopied by a wide variety of trees, including hazel. Going through a wooden gate, stop, momentarily, to glance across to the village of Wootton Courtenay and the unmistakable white church at Selworthy, high on the flanks of the hill beyond.

At this crossroads of paths, go straight on for Pitt Bridge. Through a gate and at the next signpost, turn right and go through a five-bar gate. This public bridleway to Timberscombe clings to the right-hand side of the field.

Go through a further wooden gate and on to a stony track which descends and bends right. Buildings appear on the left as you approach Bickham Farm.

Follow 'Public Bridleway' signs until reaching Ford Bridge and the A396 main road. Turn right and follow the road back to Timberscombe and your car.

DID YOU KNOW?

- The main road running alongside the village of Timberscombe was once a turnpike road running from Dunster to Dulverton.
- The history of the lost village of Clicket was investigated by archaeologist Mark Horton for a BBC West edition of *Inside Out* in 2008.

WALK 13:   *Exford*

Situated on the edge of the River Exe, in the heart of Exmoor, is the delightful village of Exford. This traditional setting finds the majority of buildings, including a post office, shops and hotel, surrounding a village green.

The walk begins at the church and takes you north of the village, passing through deserted farmsteads at Prescott. Now long gone with what remains in a state of disrepair, this location was once a settlement split into two farms – namely Lower and Higher Prescott. Each possessed its own tiny quarry, the source of building materials. As the nineteenth century drew to a close, the farm land had been lost and the dwellings were utilised as farm labourers' cottages. But later in the next century, the properties were finally abandoned.

Up over fields, the walk returns to the village via a tarmaced track. Before returning to your car, take a moment to stroll around. On a fine day, you can enjoy refreshments in the courtyard garden of Exford Bridge Tea Rooms. Or, if it's something a little stronger you're after, pop in to one of the inns. For children, the village boasts a play area.

Distance: 3.25 km/2 miles approx. | Time: 1½ hours approx., with young children | Parking and starting point: Roadside parking outside St. Mary Magdalene Church on the edge of Exford (grid ref: SS 857 385) Toilets at start: None | Difficulties: Plenty of easy walking with few climbs. The steepest section is on road from the centre of Exford village back to your car. Map: Explorer map OL9

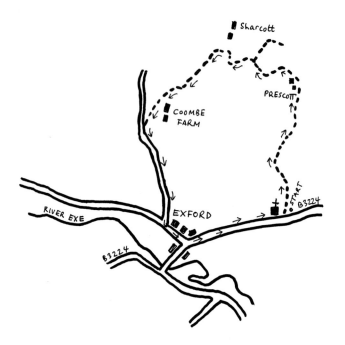

THE WALK

Look for a gate at the side entrance to the church grounds. Here, you'll also see a public footpath sign at a five-bar gate. Go through, and a second gate, following the sign for 'Prescott ½'.

The track runs alongside a field. On reaching a split, keep right and clamber over a stile at the side of a metal gate; you'll also notice the yellow waymark, one of many on this walk.

The track gradually drops and bends left, with a stream joining briefly on the right. After traversing it via a short footbridge, go through a wooden gate and turn right for Prescott. The path is flanked by high-sided banks as it runs along a field boundary to another wooden gate. Don't go through: instead, bear left up a track, again running adjacent to a fence, until reaching another

The start of the walk at Exford church

wooden five-bar gate, left of a stone dwelling.

Go through the gate, continuing towards Prescott. Cross a footbridge over a stream and go over a stile. A short climb up a field brings you to a large tree and another stile. Once over, follow the footpath sign and head for trees in the middle of the next field, again looking out for yellow waymarks.

On reaching the stand of trees, continue across the field to a further stile, beside a metal gate. Keep left over the stile, against the tree border. After around 27 m (30 yards), look for a metal gate on your left. Enter and go down to another metal gate. Go through and you'll reach the dilapidated stone buildings that once formed Prescott – formerly the site of two farms – lying in a small valley.

Ignore the path bending left as you approach the first derelict building. Continue up a slight incline, between the old dwellings, looking out for a yellow arrow on a tree. Bear left.

At the next signpost, bend right, signed 'Prescott Down ½'. Follow the field boundary, on your left, up over the field to a wooden gate. Go through and head in the direction of 'Exford

The early stages of the walk at Exford

via Coombe Farm'. Straight ahead, ensuring you keep right of the treed field boundary, marked 'Public Footpath Exford'.

Walk down over the field, through a wooden gate and over a stepped stile before turning right, keeping snug to another treed boundary with a partly obscured farmhouse ahead of you.

On reaching a fence, turn left and walk down the field, towards the sound of running water, the source of which is hidden by trees. Reaching a wooden signpost on your right, pointing back up the field, head down towards a telegraph pole and wooden footbridge.

Cross the bridge and turn immediately left. Walk to the next wooden five-bar gate, keeping the stream on your left. Go through the gate and with the stream remaining on your left, continue towards a stone house ahead.

Don't go through the next wooden five-bar gate. Instead, turn right and follow a fence. Reaching another wooden gate, go through, passing Coombe Farm and a stone dwelling on your left; enjoy the view across fields towards Exford before passing through a metal gate and joining a track. Turn left.

The village of Exford

Follow the tarmaced track, ignoring a path on your right for Edgecott and a road on the left for Coombe Farm. Continue down to Exford. Houses will soon appear on both sides; beware of cars on this narrow track.

Meeting a T-junction, with the children's play area ahead, turn left on to Park Street. There is no pavement so take care walking towards Exford's post office and The Exmoor Stores, on the left.

At the junction, with the Crown Hotel immediately left, turn left. It isn't ideal to finish a walk with a climb but, unfortunately, that is what faces you as you head up Church Hill, passing Exford's Memorial Hall on the right, to your car. Thankfully, it's shortlived.

DID YOU KNOW?

- In the nineteenth century, iron and copper mines were present in the vicinity.
- The church, dating back to the fifteenth century, is home to a decorative rood screen, a fine piece of craft work, over 500 years old. It once stood in St Audries' Church, some 32 km (20 miles) away.

Around Countisbury

This short walk is ideal for the days you're pushed for time or simply fancy stretching your legs without being out for hours. Plus, it's an ideal walk with children because it's not too long and offers plenty of varied scenery to keep them interested.

Before the A39, which runs down the south-west of England, descends the steep Countisbury Hill into Lynmouth, you'll reach the hilltop settlement of Countisbury. A church, inn, car park and cluster of houses make up this tiny parish, the name of which translates, it's believed, as 'fort on the hill', after the Iron Age fort on nearby Wind Hill.

The walk circles the quiet hamlet and joins, briefly, the long-distance South West Coast Path (see 'Introduction' for details of this long-distance walk). Fine views are everywhere, but none better than when you stare down on heavily-wooded Watersmeet, one of Britain's deepest river gorges and home to a quaint National Trust-owned nineteenth-century tea room with picturesque gardens. Sadly, it's not on the agenda for this walk.

Sheep grazing near Countisbury

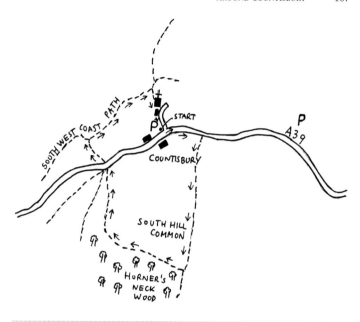

Distance: 2.5 km/1½ miles approx. | Time: 40 mins approx. (with children) | Parking and starting point: Car park opposite The Blue Ball Inn (grid ref: SS 746 496). Free but National Trust box for contributions. This car park is jointly owned by the National Trust and the inn so at busy times, park in the free car park further up the road, on the left, meaning you'll have to walk down the road to begin the walk | Toilets at start: None | Difficulties: An easy route with little in the way of steepness, just a few short stretches | Map: Explorer map OL9

THE WALK

After parking, turn left at the car park entrance and head up the hill. Walk approx. 75 m (80 yards), taking great care because it's a windy and narrow stretch of road. Reaching a sign on the right, follow in the direction of 'Watersmeet 1 via Trilly Ridge',

TOP *Near Countisbury, looking down towards Watersmeet*
ABOVE *Walking along Winston's Path near Countisbury*

through a wooden five-bar gate and along a track.

After three more five-bar gates, enter a field and follow a wooden sign marked 'Watersmeet ¾'. As the field begins to slope away, look for a post showing you're on track. The field drops steeply to a wooden gate. Once through, turn right and follow in the direction of the sign, 'Winston's Path – Countisbury ½'.

The path runs along the top of a steep-sided gorge, through a dense wooded area largely consisting of oak trees. Take care, especially if it's wet or you're walking with children.

After climbing some wooden steps, you'll reach a gate. The path climbs briefly beyond the gate before levelling. The view opens out and the sound of water far below in Watersmeet, where the East Lyn river and Farley Water converge, can be heard.

Eventually, you'll catch sight of the A39 while the path bears right and leads towards the road, descending steeply briefly. Bear left for Lynmouth, passing a small pond on the right. When the path forks, keep right and walk uphill to a wooden gate. Take care because the gate opens on to the road.

Cross the road and your route is signified by a wooden sign stating 'Permitted Footpath Coast Path Lynmouth'. Go through two wooden gates and up over the field, keeping close to the stone wall. When the field boundary turns right to a gate, follow the sign, 'Coast Path Lynmouth'. Almost immediately after the gate, you pick up the famous 1014 km (630-mile) South West Coast Path – running from Minehead in Somerset to Poole in Dorset – for a short time.

Head straight on but don't hurry, the views from this spot are spectacular and worth savouring. To your right, rocky Foreland Point, straight ahead the Bristol Channel and to your left the jagged coastline running to Lynmouth and beyond.

The path has a slight incline as it continues, staying close to the stone wall. Before long, the car park, church and Countisbury's Blue Ball Inn appear on your right.

When the stone wall ends, ignore the path continuing and

bear right, climbing briefly and rejoining the stone wall. On approaching the church, look for a gate on the right, leading through the churchyard and around to the front of the church. At the front gate, turn right on to a track and return to the car park, approx. 45 m (50 yards) on your right.

If you've parked up the hill, turn left on meeting the A39 and walk up until you reach a turning on the left, forming the entrance to the parking area.

DID YOU KNOW?

- Winston's Path was named after Winston Singleton, who for over three decades was the warden at Watersmeet and helped build the path in the 1970s.
- The Watersmeet area, where you'll find one of the largest surviving ancient woodlands of south-west England, was a site for industry in the nineteenth and early twentieth centuries. Attempts to extract iron ore were unsuccessful while the East Lyn river became home to one of Britain's first hydro-electric stations. It provided electric to Lynmouth and Lynton before the horrific floods of 1952 washed it away.

WALK 15:   *Lynton – The Valley of Rocks*

This walk takes us into a magical corner of Exmoor, a popular tourist attraction with an evocative name: the Valley of Rocks. It sounds like the setting for one of those gory 1970s movies where dinosaurs roam the land and pterodactyls circle high above.

Whether arriving at the Valley – just a mile from the hilltop town of Lynton – on foot or by car, the first thing which hits you is how different the landscape is to the rest of Exmoor: a secret world, tucked away under the shelter of surrounding hills. The jagged, spiky rocks with such intriguing names as Castle Rock, Ragged Jack, Chimney Rock and Devil's Cheesewring are just another factor in the contrasting make-up of Exmoor.

The walk begins in Lynton and travels along the South West Coast Path on a stretch called North Walk, offering fine coastal views all the way to the Valley of Rocks. Plenty of time should be allowed to wander and explore the Valley before returning to Lynton via a pleasant path, keeping you off the road.

Don't leave the area before looking around Lynton and Lynmouth, which bestrides the confluence of two rivers: the West and East Lyn. If you're tired after your walk, travel down to Lynmouth on the water-powered funicular railway connecting the twin towns. Opened in 1890, it has become a major tourist attraction.

The cliffs posed problems when freight had to be transported up to Lynton, the only methods available being horse and cart or packhorse up the steep hill; plus, tourists began flocking to Lynmouth in the 1820s on paddle steamers, and faced a daunting challenge just to reach Lynton. Now, that challenge has disappeared thanks to the railway, which runs on 263 m (862 feet) of track.

Strolling around Lynmouth, with its array of Victorian buildings, many adorned with Swiss-style balconies, it's easy to see why it's been dubbed 'Little Switzerland'.

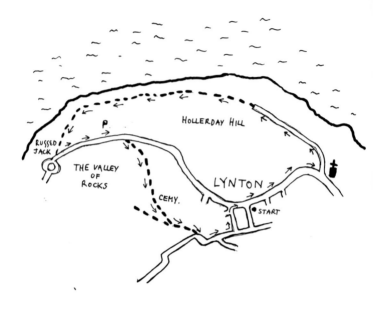

Distance: 3.5 km/2¼ miles approx. | Time: 1¼ hours approx. (with children) | Parking and starting point: There is restricted parking in Lynton's main street or unrestricted street parking in some side roads, like the one we chose (grid ref: SS 716 493). Alternatively, there is a pay-and-display car park | Toilets at start: Next to Tourist Information in Lynton | Difficulties: This is an easy walk, but take great care with small children when approaching the Valley of Rocks along the coast path. Also, the path climbs gradually for a time on leaving the Rocks | Map: Explorer map OL9

THE WALK

Wherever you park your car in Lynton, make your way to the Parish Church of St Mary the Virgin, where this walk begins. From here, turn into North Walk Hill, a no-through road. When the pavement ends, continue in the direction of the black sign for 'Valley of Rocks', carrying the acorn symbol of the South West Coast Path, which we'll follow to the Rocks.

Continue past the North Cliff Hotel and Chough's Nest Hotel on the narrow tarmaced road which soon becomes a tarmaced path, running all the way around a steep, treed hillside. On the right, it's soon a severe drop into the Bristol Channel – fine views are on offer, though.

Pass through a wooden gate, with another sign showing 'Public Footpath Valley of Rocks ¼'. There are plenty of benches, just in case you want to rest and admire the sea views or look back

Looking down on the Tors Hotel, Lynmouth, with Foreland Point in the background

towards craggy Foreland Point.

The path twists around the coast and reaches a split. For a short detour, turn left, signed 'Lynton/Holler Day Hill'. Up on the right, above some seats, you gain a fine vantage point for photos – take care, though.

Returning to the signpost at the split, turn left, signed 'Coast Path Castle Rock'. On reaching another wooden sign, by seats on the left, you'll leave the coast path and take a stony, uneven track bending to the left up to a car park. But before you do, ensure you explore this spectacular landform, a former river valley running parallel to the coastline instead of towards it in the normal fashion.

At the car park, you'll join the road and pass Mother Meldrum's Tea Gardens and Restaurant, a wonderful setting for an establishment – the Devonshire cream tea and Ragged Jack

LEFT *The Valley of Rocks*
BELOW *The cricket pitch at the Valley of Rocks is arguably the most picturesque setting for any wicket*

scones (named after one of the rocks) are highly recommended. Links with R.D. Blackmore's *Lorna Doone* are present here, too, because Mother Meldrum is the name of a witch-cum-soothsayer in his famous Exmoor-based novel.

Continue up the road, keeping to the grass verge, and just before reaching the gated entrance to Lynton and Lynmouth Cricket Club, arguably the most spectacular setting for a wicket in the entire British Isles, cross and shoot up the grassy track, signed 'Public footpath Lynton ¾'. This path keeps you off the road as you return to Lynton.

The path climbs gradually, passing a public toilet block on the left, before going through a wooden gate and trees after which it levels out. Soon, you'll pass a cemetery on your left and the houses of Lynton will come into view. Keep high when the path splits

Lynmouth

because the left-hand route leads down to the cemetery.

Continue ahead on meeting a path (travelling to Lee Abbey and Lee Bay via South Cleave, some 3.25 km/2 miles away) veering off on your right. Our route starts to climb slowly again and bends to the right, joining a tarmaced narrow lane, known as Lydiate Lane or the County Road.

Turn down the lane, marked 'Lynton via County Road'. It drops steeply and bends left. When you meet a main road at Station Hill, on a sharp bend, continue down the hill, passing a children's play area and bowling green on the left. Follow the road around to the left into Crossmead. At the end of the road, turn right on to Lee Road, where Lynton's shops begin and walk back to your car.

But before you jump in your vehicle, why not extend your day in the area and explore Lynmouth, situated below Lynton? You can either walk down or jump on the Cliff Railway.

Lynmouth was devastated in 1952 by the forces of nature after torrential rain led to cascading torrents of water rushing down from the moors, wreaking havoc and causing substantial loss of life. Today, the Lyn rivers are at peace as they meet at Lynmouth and flow out to sea.

DID YOU KNOW?

- Wild goats roam the Valley of Rocks. The current herd are Cheviots from Northumberland and were brought here in 1976. They replaced the feral goats which had a presence here for centuries.
- The Valley of Rocks has many literary links. In the late eighteenth century, poets Coleridge and Wordsworth were visitors. Impressed by what they saw, they proceeded to set 'The Wanderings of Cain' in the valley. Sadly, the work was never finished.

At the head of one of England's deepest valleys, the charming Hunter's Inn acts as a focal point for visitors to this dramatic section of Exmoor. Whether you're a walker or here for a simple wander along the deep wooded valley, you can't fail to be impressed by your surroundings.

The inn began life in the mid-nineteenth century with beer being sold from the kitchen, but in the 1890s the then thatched property was severely damaged by fire; over the following years, it was repaired and has remained largely unchanged to this day.

This route encompasses many facets. Beginning with a walk down one side of Heddon Valley, a lush wooded river valley boasting many side combes and scree, we continue along the coast on an exposed but spectacular path, above some of England's highest sea cliffs, before taking a quick detour to see the remains of a Roman fortlet dating back to the first century AD.

Continuing along, you'll eventually spot Woody Bay, nestling among the gigantic cliffs and hanging oakwoods. Now quiet, it was destined to become a thriving holiday resort, or so its owner, Colonel Lake, hoped when he acquired it in the 1880s. A pier was built to bring in the tourists but it wasn't long enough to enable visitors to disembark at low tide. Before the century was out, storms had badly damaged the ill-fated construction and, in 1902, it was finally demolished.

The walk can be extended to include an amble down to Woody Bay. But my route turns and heads back to Hunter's Inn via Martinhoe, a peaceful hamlet, near where Hollow Brook evolves into, arguably, one of Britain's highest waterfalls, tumbling some 200 m (656 feet) to the sea in several stages, including two 50-m (164-foot) drops.

After the dramatic coastal landscapes during the first stage of the walk, the return is largely dominated by a soft pastoral scene before reaching a steep road descending to our starting point.

*Distance: 7.25 km/4½ miles approx. | Time: 2 hours approx. |
Parking and starting point: Roadside near Hunter's Inn or in the
National Trust car park. £1 donations requested. (grid ref: SS 655
481) | Toilets at start: Next to National Trust shop | Difficulties:
The first half of the walk includes a gentle climb but the return leg
contains a steep descent on the road back to Hunter's Inn | Map:
Explorer map OL9*

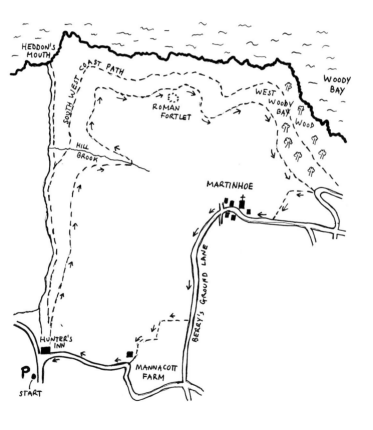

THE WALK

Facing Hunter's Inn, look for a road sign on an incline to the right of the inn. As the road bends sharp right, continue straight ahead on a wide footpath marked 'Public Bridleway Heddon's Mouth, Public Footpath Woody Bay 2¾'.

About 70 m (80 yards) later, the path splits. Take the right-hand fork, marked 'Footpath Woody Bay', heading up through Roar Wood; down on your left, you'll see the babbling River Heddon running towards Heddon's Mouth.

The route climbs steadily through trees but eventually you'll leave them behind. As you bend around a steep and deep combe, with Hill Brook running through it towards the River Heddon, take a moment to admire the views.

Walking eastwards, away from Heddon's Mouth

The path bends back at the head of the combe, crossing Hill Brook, and then sweeps to the right, with glorious open sea views in both directions, including all the way to Foreland Point, along the coast from Lynmouth. Below, you'll notice another track – this is the South West Coast Path.

Watch for a wooden sign on your right, directing you to a viewpoint and Roman fortlet. It's a brief detour up a steep, narrow path which can be slippery when wet. The path bends back on itself and you'll need to climb some wooden steps built within a gap in a stone wall. Coastal erosion over the centuries means the remains are situated close to the edge. The earthworks have a circumference of around 80 m (262 feet) and were excavated in the 1960s.

Retrace your steps to the main path, turning right and continuing along the track. Occasional benches are situated along the walk; it doesn't matter which one you choose for a rest because they're all in perfect settings to admire the view, listen to the waves crashing against the rocky coastline below and to hear the gulls screaming as they swoop close to the water. If you're lucky, during the walk you might even catch sight of, among others, ravens, razorbills or wood warblers.

The path bends around another combe, in which Hollow Brook runs, and along the top of West Woody Bay Wood. Reaching a wooden five-bar gate, go through and soon you'll see Woody Bay through the trees on your left.

Reaching a tarmaced road, on a sharp bend, turn left if you want a detour down to Woody Bay. Our route, however, cuts back up on itself, following the wooden sign on the right, marked 'Public footpath Martinhoe Common ¼'. The narrow path soon reaches a tarmaced road. Turn right and walk past a road sign for Martinhoe. Ignore the wooden sign for Martinhoe Common on the left, just before the village sign.

The road bends and the buildings of Martinhoe appear, including The Old Rectory Hotel and St Martin Church on the right and the village hall immediate left. Follow the road as it

LEFT *Looking eastwards along the coast to Woody Bay and beyond*
ABOVE *Martinhoe church*

bends left by the post box, continuing along what is known as Berry's Ground Lane.

Take care leaving Martinhoe because there is no path or verge. As well as keeping your eyes and ears open for cars, look for a cut in the right-hand hedge and a wooden signpost. Head in the direction of 'Public footpath Mannacott', through a wooden five-bar gate with a yellow-capped post.

Walk down the field, keeping close to the right-hand boundary. Across the field, you'll see a wooden sign pointing back in the direction from which you've come, signed 'County Road'. At this point, the path bends left and drops down the side of the field, canopied by hedgerows.

At the bottom of this steep, rubbly path, turn right through a small yellow-marked gate and bend left, down to the edge of a brook. Turn right and walk along the path, close to the brook. Soon, you reach another five-bar gate. Go through this and another gate, the second positioned between two old stone farm

Sheep grazing in a field off Berry's Ground Lane near Martinhoe. Trentishoe Down in the distance

buildings at Mannacott Farm.

With the farmhouse in front, take the partly tarmaced track on the left, which climbs and hits the road on an exceedingly sharp bend. Turn right and walk down the hill (known as King's Lane), passing a right-hand turning, which is a private road for Heddon's Gate and Martinhoe Cleave.

Ignore any tracks on either side and remain on the tarmaced road, which steepens on the final descent to Hunter's Inn and your car.

DID YOU KNOW?

- In times gone by, secluded Heddon's Mouth was popular with smugglers.
- In the 1920s, a steamer having left Ilfracombe, further down the coast, ran into trouble when its rudder broke. Drifting out of control, it was towed to safety in the cove where the 400 passengers managed to disembark.

WALK 17:   *Trentishoe Down*

Whichever way you drive to the tiny parish of Trentishoe, you'll have to negotiate some narrow roads. But any headaches caused by edging around sharp bends and through tight lanes soon disappear on reaching this beautiful section of Exmoor, where it's believed smuggling was rife in the nineteenth century.

This walk crosses the open terrain of Trentishoe Down, where the 324-m (1,062-foot) summit is crowned by two Bronze Age barrows. It reaches a path known as Ladies' Mile (see description below) before climbing steeply, crossing a road and continuing in a westerly direction along the South West Coast Path, Britain's

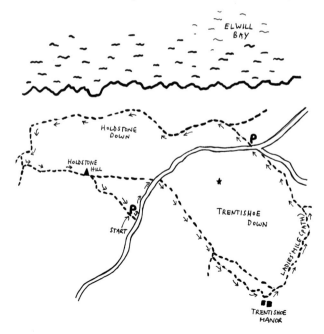

longest National Trail, for a time; the coastal views on this stretch of the walk are stunning.

Walking around the lower slopes of Holdstone Down, we return to our car via the summit of Holdstone Hill, with its large cairn.

If one was feeling energetic, the walk could easily be extended to Combe Martin, a small seaside resort on the edge of the National Park, by following the South West Coast Path down into Sherrycombe, up the other side, around the cairn atop Great Hangman – arguably the highest sea cliff on the British mainland with its face 250 m (800 feet) high – and along the coast, returning via road and track to rejoin the Coast Path at Sherrycombe.

Distance: 7 km/4¼ miles approx. | Time: 3 hours approx., with young children | Parking and starting point: Free off-road car park on the south-eastern side of Holdstone Hill. Entrance has a blue metal height barrier (grid ref: SS 623 474) | Toilets at start: None | Difficulties: Plenty of easy walking but a few climbs, especially the steep ascent from the path known as Ladies' Mile to Trentishoe Lane. There is also a steady climb to the summit of Holdstone Hill | Map: Explorer map OL9

THE WALK

From the car park entrance, turn left and walk up the tarmaced road. On the right the vast open heathland of Trentishoe Down contrasts with the undulating agricultural landscape beyond, stretching to the horizon.

Walk past a fenced field and Moorland View, a bungalow, on the right. Reaching, again on the right, a black metal barrier across the entrance of a track, just past the dwelling and opposite a car park, turn into the track. The wooden sign opposite the entrance states, 'Permitted Path Ladies' Mile'.

The wide, easy-going path cuts across the Down, carpeted in

Walking down over Trentishoe Down

heather and grass blowing in the breeze, and drops away, allowing glorious views.

When the path forks at a small wooden arrow-emblazoned post, ignore the right-hand track and continue down. Just before reaching the stone wall boundary on the right, veer off to the left; the path – much narrower now – continues to descend, retaining the field boundary on the right.

You'll reach some trees as the path becomes uneven; then, as the wood becomes denser, the path begins to twist, but still continues to drop, soon descending steeply to a wooden sign at a path junction. Turn left on to 'Ladies' Mile'.

Look back and you should catch sight of Trentishoe Manor through the trees; once a rectory, the Ladies' Mile footpath was constructed so women from the Manor could reach the local church.

This secluded and tranquil path is bordered by predominantly silver birch for some distance as it runs along the base of Trentishoe Down before bending left and around to a crossroads of paths. Turn left, uphill, signed 'Trentishoe to Coast Path'. This is the steepest part of the walk, the path bending right as it climbs and

becomes more rubbly as you reach the top, with a field on your right. Bending left, it twists its way up to a road.

At the road, you'll see a wooden sign, indicating 'Public footpath Trentishoe Church 1'. You're not going that way. Instead, turn left, on to the road and you'll reach a road sign at a junction, with a car park on the right. Go into the car park and take the track leading off the parking area, heading in a north-westerly direction.

Paths will join from left and right, near a field entrance, but carry on, keeping close to the field boundary on the right. You're heading towards Holdstone Down now. When the South West Coast Path meets you on the right at a wooden sign, carry on ahead marked 'Coast Path Combe Martin 5½'. The path bends left and climbs, affording you breathtaking views along the coast, especially back towards Heddon's Mouth.

At the next wooden sign, continue on the coast path in the direction of Combe Martin, not forgetting to admire the impressive field-capped cliffs behind you – good material for photos.

The path goes through a gap in a stone boundary cutting across your route before making a wide curve. A minor path joins on the left at a small cairn. Carry on until you join a wide path. Turn right, following an acorn-inscribed arrowed post pointing along the coast path. You'll continue for some time, looking ahead to Great Hangman and Blackstone Point.

The path bends to the left and changes back to grass, a welcome softness under weary feet. Another grassy track joins from the left. As you approach the drop into Sherrycombe, the path turns sharp left and climbs slightly before bending right, just as a minor path meets you from the left.

At a wooden sign, turn left and climb, signed 'County Road'. Soon, you'll meet a crossroads of grassy paths. Turn left (not signed) and begin your ascent on to Holdstone Hill. The path runs to the right of a tumbledown stone wall, cutting between some high gorse bushes, so mind you don't get scratched. Eventually,

Walking along the Ladies' Mile, a path at the bottom of Trentishoe Down

ABOVE *Looking along the coast from Holdstone Down*
LEFT *Delight at reaching the summit of Holdstone Hill*

you'll reach the trig point and large cairn at the top of the hill, some 349 m (1,145 feet) high.

After resting and enjoying the panoramic views, leave the summit by the exit path on the right, nearest the trig point. It bends as it descends to the car park, on the left, next to the road.

DID YOU KNOW?

- The tiny hamlet of Trentishoe gets its name from Old English, meaning spur on a rounded hillside.
- This area was the setting for nineteenth-century novelist Henry Kingsley's romantic story *Ravenshoe*, arguably the writer's best piece of work.

WALK 18: *Ralegh's Cross – Clatworthy Reservoir*

This walk, largely through fields, explores the rolling landscape and wooded valleys of the Brendon Hills which at their western extremities blend into the less cultivated uplands of Exmoor.

The route begins at Ralegh's Cross (sometimes spelt Raleigh's Cross), where a large inn stands; it was once a stopping-off point for drovers travelling from the Exe Valley to market at the county town of Taunton.

The remains of the actual cross which stood here can be found close to the inn, although it's only the base and a tiny part of its octagonal structure which have survived.

This is not a well-trodden route and crosses fields, skirts farms and descends to the northern edge of Clatworthy Reservoir, a 130-acre reservoir which impounds the headwaters of the River Tone and supplies water to around 200,000 homes in the region. It reaches a maximum depth of 29.5 m (97 feet). Building the dam began in 1957 and was completed in December 1958; it was filled during the following year. The original plans had to be amended when the announcement of Hinkley Point power station being built meant there would be a much higher demand for water.

The return leg of this walk which, eventually, heads north back up to the B3190 is equally quiet. Enjoy the solitude.

Distance: 8 km/5 miles approx. | Time: 2¼ hours approx. | Parking and starting point: Lay-by on the B3190, in between Ralegh's Cross Hotel and the B3224 turning for Wheddon Cross (grid ref: ST 033 343) | Toilets at start: None | Difficulties: Walking on a fast country road at the beginning of the route plus a few steep descents and ascents | Map: Explorer map OL9

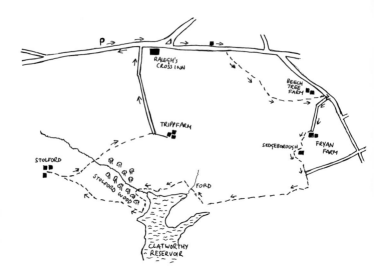

THE WALK

From your car walk along the B3190 in an easterly direction passing the Ralegh's Cross Hotel. At a junction by the hotel, carry on around the road, which becomes a continuation of the B3224

Walk for around half a mile taking great care because it's a fast road with no pavement. You'll pass dwellings on your left. Look out for a track on the right, leading to a metal field gate. The post carries a small yellow-arrowed disc indicating a footpath.

Go through the gate, turn left and walk down over the field to another metal gate positioned on the left-hand boundary. Go through and turn right, keeping the boundary close to your right now.

You'll pass through a series of fields; it's not the best marked route on Exmoor so keep your eyes peeled for the various arrowed discs which turn to blue, indicating public bridleway, as you approach Beech Tree Farm. After seeing the first blue arrowed disc, go through the gate and cross the field. Ignore the metal gate on your left and aim for a rusty gate in the field's bottom corner,

Walking across fields towards Clatworthy Reservoir

again marked by a blue arrow. Pass through and on to another gate, some 27 m (30 yards) away.

Keep high in the next field, passing a telegraph pole, house and Beech Tree Farm on the left. Go across to the corner of the field and through the metal gate, leading on to a tarmaced road at Holcombe Water.

Turn right and right again a few metres up the track, leading off the road to a wooden five-bar gate. Follow the public bridleway sign. A tarmaced track climbs gradually, levels and then drops on approaching Fryan Farm.

Ignore the track leading into the farm, keeping right to a metal gate marked with the blue bridleway arrow. You'll pass barns on the left before going through the next metal gate. Keep the hedged boundary close on the right and walk down over the field to a gate in the far corner. Go through and down over another field, bending right.

Through a further two metal gates at which point the buildings of Sedgeborough appear on the left. Just before the next metal

OVERLEAF *Looking down on the northern edge of Clatworthy Reservoir*

gate, turn left (look for the small blue arrowed disc on the tree) and take the gravel track skirting the buildings before twisting and rising to a metal gate. Go through and at a junction of paths, turn right and then, immediately, straight ahead into a field beyond the metal fence. Turn left in the direction of the arrow.

Keep close to the left-hand boundary walking down the field to a metal gate. Don't go through; instead, turn right and with the treed boundary close on the left, walk over to a small five-bar gate. Once through, head across the next field to a metal gate. Go through.

Now you'll see the northern edge of Clatworthy Reservoir in front of you. Keep high in the following field (which falls away steeply), close to the boundary. At the far end you'll meet a wire fence with a gate in the left-hand corner carrying a bridleway arrow. We're not going in this direction: our route turns right and descends alongside the fence. Take care because it's very steep, the surface is unsteady and slippery, particularly in wet conditions.

At a metal gate in the bottom of the field, go through and cross the ford, walking up to another metal gate. Climb up over the field, with Clatworthy Reservoir to your left. Before reaching the large tree in the middle of the field above you, turn to your left. There isn't a discernible path but keep right of the ferns and drop towards an ungated entrance. Follow the public bridleway sign into the next field and down towards the reservoir.

The route bends right and follows a fence on the left. Look for a small gate and wooden footbridge on the left. Cross the bridge and walk up to a large five-bar wooden gate. Don't go through, keep right and follow the bridleway sign, climbing through trees on the edge of Stolford Wood.

The path bends left and continues to a small five-bar gate. Go through and turn left, keeping close to a wire fence. At the next wooden gate, go through; breaks in the trees mean you can enjoy views of the reservoir once again.

Before long, the path bends to the right and you'll see a wooden post sporting a public bridleway sign. Walk up over the field, which is particularly steep initially before levelling out somewhat. Near the crest of the rise, look for another bridleway marker on a fence post to your left.

Walk to the metal gate in the left-hand corner of the field. Once through, go up over the next field, keeping tight to the treed left-hand boundary. Reaching the top, you'll notice a gate on the left carrying a bridleway arrow. Disregard it and continue to the gate after a small fenced off area. Go through and another gate straight after. Walk down the wide and, at times, muddy track to a further gate, with farm barns on the right. Once through, immediately turn right back on yourself and enter the wooden five-bar gate, following the bridleway sign.

The path runs close to a wire fence and drops to a split. Turn left and go through the wooden gate into a field. Drop down to a metal gate. Go through, cross a stream and bend right, climbing up through trees. Take no notice of a track joining from the left.

When the path splits, ignore the right-hand direction descending through trees. Your route is steep up to a small five-bar gate which was broken the last time I completed the walk. Go through and walk up over the field to a wooden gate (ignoring a metal one on the right). Go through and keep close to the treed border on the right as you walk to a metal gate. Once through, turn left on to a track (occasionally tarmaced) which you stay on for just under a mile until reaching the B3190, left of Ralegh's Cross Hotel. Turn left and walk back to your car in the lay-by, taking care once again due to the speed of traffic flowing along this road.

DID YOU KNOW?

- Clatworthy Reservoir offers anglers the chance to fish for rainbow and brown trout. The biggest rainbow trout ever caught weighed in at nearly 17 lb in 1998. Four years earlier, a brown trout at just over 8 lb was pulled from the water.
- The building of the reservoir meant the flooding of Syndercombe, an ancient settlement.

WALK 19: *Robber's Bridge – Oare*

When I was young, family trips on to Exmoor from our home in Minehead would occasionally end up at Robber's Bridge, where we'd toss stones into the water, explore the riverbank and enjoy a picnic. There was something mystical about the name, conjuring up images in my mind of adventures in days gone by when highwaymen were on the prowl.

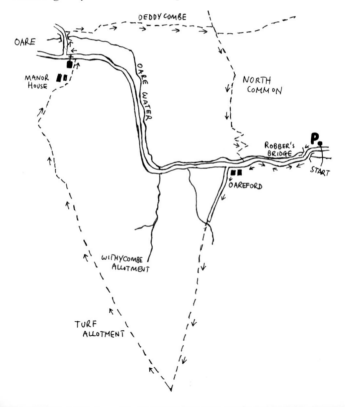

Robber's Bridge, crossing Weir Water, isn't one of the prettiest bridges on Exmoor but it's wrapped in legend and intrigue: it's supposedly where a Doone robbery took place and has a reputation, rightly or wrongly, for being bandit territory in centuries past. Furthermore, the fact it's reached down a narrow, wooded road, off the A39, adds to the magic of this popular beauty spot.

This walk crosses the arch bridge and heads west on a road before cutting up into fields at Oareford, climbing Stowey Ridge until turning in a north-westerly direction down to Oare, via Oare Common.

Oare is famous largely for its church, where John Ridd and Lorna Doone tied the knot in R.D. Blackmore's famous novel. It's an isolated settlement with no post office, shop or facilities but boasts a pleasant eighteenth-century road bridge crossing Oare Water.

The return leg of the walk climbs steeply before crossing the wide open space of North Common and zig-zagging back down to the road and the car park nearby.

Distance: 9 km/5½ miles approx. | Time: 2¾ hours approx. | Parking and starting point: Car park alongside Weir Water, near Robber's Bridge (grid ref: SS 821 464) | Toilets at start: None | Difficulties: There are sharp climbs both sides of the valley and the descent during the final stage of the walk is relatively steep | Map: Explorer map OL9

THE WALK

From the car park, turn right and walk along the road, crossing Robber's Bridge. Continue down the road with Weir Water running on your right, fields on the left. The road bends right and left and goes over another bridge and past two dwellings on the left, including the Old School House, in what is Oareford.

Sheep grazing on Stowey Ridge near Oareford

Once past the stone house, turn immediately left, up a wide, stony path, signed 'Public bridleway Stowey Bridge Larkbarrow 3'. The track passes through four metal gates. Once through the final one, a track veers off left. Ignore this and keep straight ahead, climbing close to the field boundary. The views are sublime: to your left, across to Mill Hill and, behind you, back towards North Common, close to the A39.

On reaching another metal gate, go through. You'll now face three tracks: ignore the right and middle options, choosing the left-hand track instead, which continues up over the field – this is Stowey Ridge.

Keep the fenced field boundary close on your left and continue until meeting another metal gate. Go through and carry on ahead, over another field and on to the next gate. The track's route is less clear now and there is a slight gradient, but it's easy walking with fine, open views and affords you a true sense of space.

At the next metal gate, don't go through but turn almost back on yourself and follow the sign for Oare. Look for another wooden sign at the fence in the distance, right of a row of trees.

Lonely tree on Withycombe Allotment above Oare

Walk across. Rather than going through the metal gate and out on to Turf Allotment, which is Open Access land, keep right of the boundary, following the sign for 'Oare Church'.

Eventually, you'll pass through a wooden five-bar gate with the blue bridleway marking. Continue, but you'll soon be walking to the left of the boundary, bordered by Withycombe Allotment, a carpet of heather, on your right and Oare Common on the left.

Go through another wooden gate into a field and straight ahead, staying left of the fenced boundary. Now there is a fine view up over Cloud Allotment. Reaching a metal gate, go through and, again, keep straight ahead. In the corner of the field, you'll notice a wooden sign. Continue heading in the direction of Oare Church.

Walk past some metal water troughs in the field and through a metal gate. There is a sign to the left of the gate, signing 'Oare Church' in another direction but our route goes down over the field, veering to the left and reaching a metal gate and wooden sign for Oare. Go through and across the field, dropping into the far corner and up over a bank to a wooden gate and sign. Follow

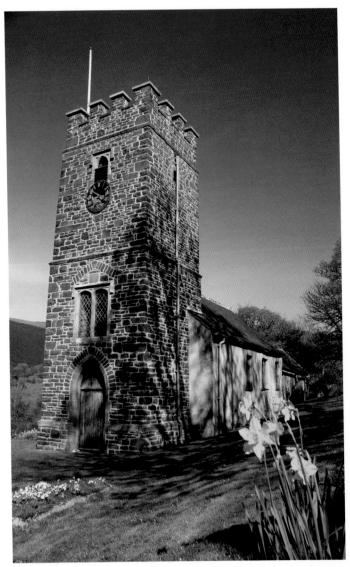

Oare Church, made famous by the novel Lorna Doone

in the direction of 'Bridleway Oare ¼', through the gate, keeping close to the fence on your left.

You'll see a bungalow to the right, beyond the bottom of the field you're crossing. As you approach, a sign on the left directs you across to a wooden five-bar gate. Follow the bridleway sign, avoiding the private garden of Oare Manor. Reaching a wooden gate at the end of the field, go through on to the road, turning left. You're now in Oare with its church on the left, made famous by the ever-popular novel *Lorna Doone*. It's worth a visit.

Coming out of the church gate, you'll notice a road sign at a junction. Turn right, signed 'Lynmouth 6¼, Porlock 7'. Go over the road bridge and as the road bends, turn right through a metal gate, signed 'Public footpath'. Take heed of the warning sign, stating that dogs must be kept on leads between 1 March and 31 July because of ground-nesting birds.

Walk along the riverbank, to the left of Oare Water, until you reach a wooden post on your right, advising all footpaths go off

Looking across while descending from North Common near Oareford

to the left. So, turn and climb up to the right of a dilapidated wooden chalet. At a sign, go right for 'Footpath North Common ¾'. It's a hard slog now, climbing up the side of Deddy Combe.

As you reach the end of the steep climb, you'll come to a small wooden five-bar gate with the familiar yellow footpath mark. Go through and follow the sign for 'Footpath North Common'. Over tussocky grass, running to the left of the field boundary, head towards a clump of trees.

When you reach a crossroads of paths, ignore the deep-rutted track leading to a metal gate on the right and continue straight on. Soon, you'll reach a track running across yours while ahead a stile crosses into a small plantation. Nearby, a wooden bench – donated by the London Area branch of the Exmoor Society in 1997 – offers wonderful views for anyone wanting a rest.

We don't need to cross the stile. Our route turns right, towards Oare Church, although no need to worry because we're not ending up back there. The broad path bends right across North Common, then gently to the left. When it splits, bear left, by the small blue-capped post. Ignore a grassy track on the left and continue towards trees.

Meeting gorse bushes, the path narrows and begins winding down to the river below. Take care because it's very steep in places.

Reaching the valley bottom, go through a wooden gate and across the bridge. At the road, turn left and walk back to the car park, just past Robber's Bridge, on your left.

DID YOU KNOW?
- The church at Oare dates from the fifteenth century.
- Weir Water begins near Lucott Cross, close to the road heading to Exford from the A39, and runs into Oare Water.

This peaceful walk begins in the nineteenth-century village of Simonsbath and follows the River Barle south-east towards Withypool before heading north briefly, then turning west back to the village. Birdsong and the gentle rippling of the river passing along are likely to be the only sounds heard on this attractive route.

Among points of interest are the ruins of Wheal Eliza Cottage. The surrounding area was once mined for copper and iron ore but

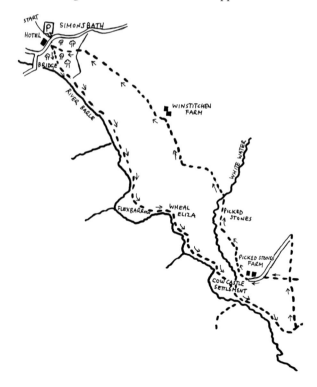

proved unprofitable and was soon abandoned. The ruins, marked by a plaque, were once a workshop and store before becoming a shepherd's cottage, last occupied in the 1950s. This spot has a grisly past: it's where the body of murdered Anna Burgess was discovered. Her father, William, committed the crime and hid his daughter's body here in the 1850s; he was later hung for his despicable crime.

Further along the outward leg of this walk, you'll pass Cow Castle, where an Iron Age fort once stood on a hillock; now, only a 2.75-m (9 foot) bank and ditch remain.

It's a rewarding walk ending back in Simonsbath, which was largely conceived after John Knight, son of a rich Shropshire industrialist, bought the King's Allotment in 1818. Wanting to turn much of the Royal Forest into agricultural land, he constructed farms within the region, enclosed large swathes of the moor and built roads.

Now, it's a quiet corner of Exmoor but popular with walkers because it's from here that a myriad of hikes begin.

Distance: 10 km/6¼ miles approx. | Time: 3 hours approx. | Parking and starting point: Ashcombe Car Park, on the right as the B3223 drops into Simonsbath. No tickets are issued but a £2 fee in the drop box is requested (grid ref: SS 774 394) | Toilets at start: At the car park | Difficulties: There are a few climbs and descents along the route but it's largely an easy walk with no particular difficulties | Map: Explorer map OL9

THE WALK

Walk out of Ashcombe car park and turn right, down the hill. When you reach The Exmoor Forest Inn on your right, cross the road. Opposite the inn is the start of our route, so follow the wooden sign marked 'Public bridleway Landacre 5 via Picked Stones 2½'. The narrow path winds up amongst the trees before dropping to a crossroads of paths and signpost. Carry straight on, signed 'MW, Two Moors Way, Cow Castle'.

The ruins of Wheal Eliza Cottage on the banks of the River Barle near Simonsbath

The path runs through trees following the 164-km (102-mile) long-distance trail, Two Moors Way, for a time; it also follows the River Barle, now on your right. The path eventually reaches a small blue-capped five-bar wooden gate. Go through.

The route becomes more open and the gentle folds of the Barle Valley appear. Ignore a path climbing up on the left, keeping straight ahead. To your left, it's a steep, grassy fern-covered bank while it's open grassland and the river meandering through the landscape on your right.

Reaching another wooden gate, go through and cross a stream. Eventually, the path bends left around Flexbarrow and you lose sight of the Barle momentarily. Approaching a grass bank with a blue-marked post, keep on the lower path to a wooden gate. Go through.

The path drops slightly and as it turns to the left, you pick up the river again. Disregard the footbridge crossing the water and carry straight on.

On the left, you'll pass what remains of the ruins of Wheal Eliza

The River Barle meanders through the countryside

Cottage and a long-forgotten mine, where the murdered body of Anna Burgess – as mentioned earlier – was discovered. Beyond the ruins you reach a wooden gate – go through. The path narrows and drops steeply – take care – before levelling out as it continues to run close to the river and a wire fence for some distance.

Go through a blue-capped gate. As the path begins to peter out, look for a blue arrow on the bark of a tree, informing you to turn left. You're taken across a short grassy area before bending right and joining the river again.

Take no notice of a small wooden gate on the left within the stone wall and proceed to another gate. Once through, your path bends left, away from the river, and rises with a wall on your left, before sweeping to the right; here, the sound of water greets you, as White Water joins the Barle. Keep to the right of White Water.

Above you at this point is what remains of Cow Castle, the circular Iron Age fort edging the River Barle which once stood atop the hillock.

The path weaves around hillocks so keep your eyes peeled for the blue bridleway waymarks *en route*.

The River Barle near Simonsbath

You'll enter a woodland plantation – running for around a third of a mile along the left-hand bank of the Barle – via a stile and wooden bridge. At a signpost, follow in the direction of 'Withypool 3½'. Go around a wooden barrier and follow the track. Eventually emerging from the cover of the trees, you'll pass through a gate. At a sign, follow in the direction of 'Public bridleway Withypool 3½ – Picked Stones'.

Out in the open again, with a steep hillside to your left, the wide track rises gently. On your right, the river is partly obscured by trees, but beyond the shapely Great Ferny Ball rises – a splendid landscape.

Eventually, you'll reach a five-bar gate. Go through. The track bends left across the field, away from the Barle. Walk across the field and through another five-bar gate. Immediately after passing through, turn left and follow the sign for 'Diverted bridleway'. It's now time to wave goodbye to the River Barle for some time.

You'll also leave behind the Two Moors Way, which continues along to Withypool. Our less defined route climbs alongside the field boundary, on your left, and finally meets a crossroads of paths. Turn left and through a five-bar gate, following for 'Simonsbath via Picked Stones'.

The path drops down to cross White Water, near the River Barle

Go straight across the field, the well-trampled, flattened grass revealing your route. Through another five-bar gate and down the tarmaced track, signed 'Bridleway Picked Stones/Simonsbath 2¾'. Go through a metal gate, ensuring you respect the landowner's request on the sign to leave the gate as found.

Reaching Picked Stones Farm, don't take the left-hand track but continue to the blue-capped post and go through a gate, following the public bridleway to Simonsbath. Through another gate and the path bends immediately right, keeping close to a bank. You'll catch glimpses of the Barle again, on the left.

Go through another wooden five-bar gate, staying close to the hedged bank, and then bend left; we're high above the Barle Valley now and the views are sumptuous.

Ignore a track and large gate on the right and continue on your route, which begins to descend. To your left, you have a clear view across the top of Cow Castle. The track drops steeply into a combe. After two metal gates, a small bridge takes you across White Water before bending right and then sharp left as it climbs steadily out of the combe.

Reaching the end of the stony track, you'll see a blue-capped post on the left. Bend left and head for a stand of trees and signpost. Continue on the bridleway to Simonsbath, with the trees now on your right. Go up over land known as Winstitchen and through into another field – walk straight across, admiring the fine rural views all around.

Pass through another five-bar gate and keep to a treed boundary. After the next gate, turn immediately right, again staying close to the right-hand boundary. Soon, you'll reach a wooden gate leading on to a hard track and the entrance to Winstitchen Farm. Don't go through. Instead, you'll see a wooden sign pointing you across the edge of the field, keeping you on the public bridleway to Simonsbath.

Follow the fence around to a blue-capped post at a wooden gate, next to an old corrugated iron barn. Go through the gate into a field, keep to the right-hand boundary while crossing the field. Through another wooden gate and straight across to a further gate. Once through, turn left, noticing the blue marker on a tree trunk. Keep close to the left-hand boundary as you wander across to a signpost by a group of trees.

At a gate, go through and follow the bridleway sign which continues ahead and through another five-bar gate, near a blue-marked water trough. Go down over the field, close to the right-hand treed boundary. After the next five-bar gate, turn left on to a track for Simonsbath and wander through a small wooded area, known as Birchcleave Wood. Ignore any minor paths on either side as you weave your way down to Simonsbath. Reaching a wooden signpost, just before the main road, turn right for 'Simonsbath Car Park, MW'. When you hit the road, turn right and walk up to Ashcombe Car Park, on the left.

DID YOU KNOW?
- By AD 1200, Exmoor was regarded as a Royal Forest and establishing any kind of settlement wasn't permitted. A farm, however, existed at Simonsbath in the seventeenth century.
- Birchcleave Wood, at 350 m (1,148 feet), is one of the highest beech woods in England.

This walk takes place in arguably the remotest and bleakest corner of Exmoor, and it's advisable to choose a bright, clear day when the last time it rained is a distant memory.

The reason is that Pinkery Pond and the immediate area known as The Chains is extremely boggy. In fact, it's a high boggy plateau and the source of several rivers, including the Barle and West Lyn. This wide expanse of peaty land resembles a gigantic sponge, absorbing rain as if there were no tomorrow! But even gigantic sponges can become deluged, which is what happened in August 1952.

The incessant rain was so torrential, this lonely plateau couldn't cope and gallons of water poured into the rivers and raced towards the sea, leaving destruction in its wake. The worst horrors were experienced north of the plateau in what became known as the Lynmouth Flood Disaster. The coastal town was devastated and thirty-six people lost their lives.

So, it's boggy, wet and a very bleak landscape with few landmarks to aid navigation in poor conditions, hence why it's best tackled in clement weather. But although it's barren, there is a mysterious quality emanating from this place, in my view; I love its remoteness, where you can be entirely alone in silence, save for the whistling wind caressing the grass.

For the first part of the walk, we head north along a stretch of the Macmillan Way West, turning left to reach our ultimate goal: Pinkery Pond, situated some 440 m (1,444 feet) above sea level. Its peat bottom is responsible for the dark, some would say eerie and foreboding appearance. Built less than 200 years ago for the Midlands' industrialist John Knight, who'd acquired the former Royal Forest of Exmoor from the Crown in the early 1800s, its purpose is unclear. Some say the pond, created by building a large earth dam across the River Barle, was to support a canal system, but, sadly, its use was never officially reported.

From Pinkery Pond, our route eventually turns south and crosses the B3358, heading for Mole's Chamber (more of that later) before turning north-east and returning back to the walk's starting point.

Distance: 9 km/5½ miles approx. | Time: 2 hours approx. | Parking and starting point: Park in a lay-by on the right of the B3358, approximately 3 miles after leaving Simonsbath (grid ref: SS 728 401) | Toilets at start: None | Difficulties: The route is primarily flat but there is a short climb at the beginning and after crossing the B3358 on the second half. It can be muddy and boggy, particularly after a rainy spell. It's a walk for a bright, dry day and best left in foggy conditions because the relatively featureless terrain can make navigating a challenge | Map: Explorer map OL9

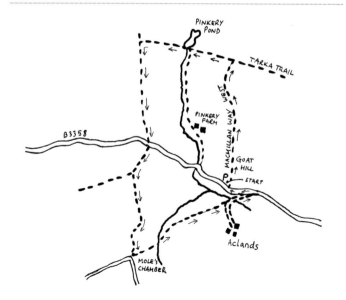

Walking up the Macmillan Way West on the Pinkery Pond walk

THE WALK

From the lay-by on the B3358, look for a wooden gate and follow the sign for 'Bridleway to Chains Barrow'. This segment of the walk is along the Macmillan Way West and ventures up over a field, with a boundary on your right.

It's a steady climb to a wire fence. Go through a gate and continue straight on over Goat Hill to another five-bar gate. Once through, follow the grassy path across the field, the nearest boundary now on your left. You'll notice another grass track crossing your path, but continue ahead; being a bridleway, the route is periodically marked by splashes of blue on posts.

Follow the marked posts across this open land while enjoying the views around you. This region's flat and featureless landscape means that on a clear day you can see for miles.

Eventually, you'll approach a wooden gate and sign at a boundary. After passing through the gate, turn left for 'Pinkery

Pinkery Pond

Pond ½'. The path continues to hug a fenced boundary on your left, but you'll find yourself having to pick your way through marshy patches *en route*.

The terrain drops away on reaching the pond, which is the ideal spot for getting your flask out. Keep your eyes open because you might catch sight of frogs in the pond.

Fully refreshed, walk around to the western side of the pond and follow the path which wriggles up. Soon, you'll meet a five-bar gate. Beyond that, the path bears right briefly before heading across open land.

Reaching a fenced boundary in front of you with a five-bar wooden gate to your right, turn left on the path, following the sign for 'B3358 Road'. You've now joined the Tarka Trail, running south across Broad Mead, through a boundary which no longer has a gate. The track, however, isn't particularly clear at times.

Take a moment to relish the expansive views either side. To your left, you'll notice the solitary wind turbine at the Pinkery

At a junction on the Tarka Trail, on the slopes of Roosthitchen, the other side of the B3358 from Pinkery Pond

Farm Exploration Centre. This ex-Victorian farmstead is owned by Exmoor National Park Authority but offers group accommodation via the Youth Hostel Association; it's also regularly used by local schools for field trips, providing youngsters with a taste of remoteness.

Our track eventually reaches a series of animal pens, and after going through a five-bar gate you're at the side of the B3358. Be careful because it can be a fast road. Cross and join the path opposite, going through another gate and following the sign for 'Public bridleway Mole's Chamber 1'.

After a small wooden gate, the track climbs to a signpost. Again, head for Mole's Chamber, keeping the wire fence close to your left. At the next sign, by a field boundary, continue on the bridleway, with the fence boundary now on your right.

The path drops down to two gates. Take the right-hand gate and go across rough pasture, after which the path runs close to a boundary stone at the head of Lew Combe and Sloley Stone. Reaching the corner of a lane, turn and pass the area known as Mole's Chamber.

The path crosses a stream and makes its way to a small wooden gate. Enter and follow the narrow path running up against the wire fence before twisting away and picking up the blue-capped waymarks.

The path runs above the marshy valley of Great Vintcombe, and to your left you'll spot the B3358 and the lay-by where you left your car.

Eventually, a wider track joins from the right. Turn left and walk down to a five-bar gate. Once through, continue to another five-bar gate, where you join a concrete track. Turn left and go down the hill. Cross the bridge and stroll up to another gate, after which you meet the road again. Turn left and walk carefully back to your car, on the right.

DID YOU KNOW?

- Mole's Chamber is supposedly named after the Reverend Mole who, according to legend, disappeared, along with his horse, into a bog.
- This area marks the point where the deepest peat (3.5 m/11½ feet) on Exmoor is found. A sixteenth-century map records the area as a dangerous bog.

WALK 22: *Tarr Steps – Knaplock*

Tarr Steps, situated 4 kilometes (2½ miles) south-east of Withypool, is one of Exmoor's most visited spots. In peak holiday periods the narrow roads leading to this ancient clapper bridge and the delightful woodland surrounding the area can become congested.

On making your first visit, you'll soon realise why people flock here. But don't let the relative busyness put you off because there are always quiet times, even in high season, when you can find yourself all alone on the clapper bridge or walking the paths.

Clapper bridges are constructed using unmortared slabs of rock resting on each other and this splendid seventeen-span specimen at Tarr Steps, crossing the River Barle, is regarded as the

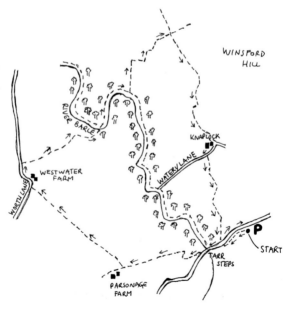

longest in Britain. A Grade I listed building, it has on a couple of occasions been damaged by storms, including the ferocious rains of 1952 which resulted in the tragic events of the Lynmouth Flood Disaster.

The woodlands around the Barle Valley are of special scientific interest and home to a host of wildlife, including deer, dormice, bats and otters. You'll explore a section of the wood on this walk which beginning at Tarr Steps spends most of its time above the Barle Valley, crossing a lush patchwork of fields before dropping down to the water and climbing on to the lower slopes of Winsford Hill on the way back to Tarr Steps via the tiny settlement of Knaplock.

It's a varied trek through woodland, across fields, along the course of a river and around open moorland; and it's just one of many walks originating from Tarr Steps.

Distance: 9.25 km/5¾ miles approx. | Time: 3 hours approx. | Parking and starting point: Park in the Exmoor National Park/West Somerset Council-run pay-and-display car park, just up the hill from Tarr Steps (grid ref: SS 872 323) | Toilets at start: At the car park | Difficulties: This is a relatively easy walk in terms of gradient but care must be taken when crossing the River Barle at grid reference SS 853 335. This is perhaps best undertaken in the summer when the river level should be at its lowest, although even then you may have to remove boots and socks. Use your judgement on reaching the water | Map: Explorer map OL9

THE WALK

From the car park, turn left and walk down the road or, alternatively, keep off the road by using the footpath running alongside, accessed from the car park. Pass Tarr Farm inn and restaurant on the right and continue down to the small roundabout at the foot of the hill.

Checking the sign to the right of the roundabout, walk across the clapper bridge in the direction of 'Public bridleway Parsonage Farm/Westwater Farm'.

Once over, ignore the track turning immediately right along the riverbank and walk a few steps before veering right on to a narrow rising track, signed 'Public bridleway Withypool Hill 3, Hawkridge 2'. The track bends right. Reaching a wooden five-bar gate marking a private drive, bear right by the blue-capped post and walk up the stony track, which is canopied by trees.

The rubbly track climbs steeply, passing three wooden gates: one on the left, two on the right. If it's the correct season, look for the splash of bluebells among the trees on the left.

At the next wooden five-bar gate, go through. Almost immediately, the track turns sharp right, edged by a moss-covered stone wall. As you reach the edge of the field, you'll notice wooden gates in front and to the right. Look for the blue arrow painted on a stone next to the gate ahead of you, telling you to turn left and follow the small track leading up the field. Look behind as you do for the fine view across to Ashway Side.

At the top of the field, ignore the wooden gate on the right and choose the one in front of you, again indicated by the public bridleway blue mark. You'll also see a green sign advertising refreshments at Parsonage Farm guesthouse and restaurant.

The path runs close to the left-hand treed border in the field to another five-bar gate. Go through, leaving the gate as you find it, in accordance with the landowner's instructions. Keep close to the left-hand border; you can't really miss your route because it's rutted, thanks to farm use. Enjoy the view to your left, across fields to South Barton Wood.

As the track drops to a gate, marking the entrance to Parsonage Farm, you'll notice a wooden signpost on the left. Turn right for 'Withypool Hill'. The rutted track runs up over the field, close to the left-hand boundary. You'll soon reach two gates: ignore the one on the left, leading on to farm land; instead, go through the other gate and continue down over a field, against the left-hand boundary. All around there are wonderful views of woods, fields and hills.

Eventually, the track reaches an ungated entrance. Go through into the next field. The route continues, this time following the right-hand boundary. Through a wooden five-bar gate and at the end of the field, you'll see a wooden sign on your left, next to a metal gate. Carry straight on, marked 'Bridleway Withypool 2'.

The track runs between trees and a wire fence before descending gradually; ahead, you'll catch sight of Westwater Farm, a 103-hectare working farm with a flock of Exmoor Horn sheep.

The path narrows as it runs between gorse bushes and stunted trees. Then, at a metal gate, go through and follow in the direction of 'Westwater Farm 0.1'. Go across the next field, keeping left of the large trees, to another metal gate. Once through, you'll meet a road. Turn right, in the direction of 'Withypool via road 1½'.

For a short time, you'll be walking along the Exe Valley Way,

BELOW *Walking through the woods near Tarr Steps*
OVERLEAF *Tarr Steps*

which heads up Worth Lane. Follow the lane over the bridge and sweep left past Westwater Farm on the right. It's a high-banked, narrow lane so beware of vehicles.

On reaching a track on your right, opposite the entrance to a house, turn right signed 'Public footpath Withypool 2½, Winsford Hill 2, Tarr Steps 2½, Ford – no bridge'.

Take note of those last three words because once stepping-stones helped you cross the River Barle but they were washed away in the terrible storm which culminated in the Lynmouth Flood Disaster of 1952. As mentioned in the 'Difficulties' section, you'll have to make a judgement on reaching the river whether to cross safely. If in any doubt, turn back.

Follow the stony, high-banked track through a metal gate towards a corrugated iron barn; at this point, look for a small wooden bridleway sign on the left, just before the barn.

The bridleway runs down to a small wooden gate and into a field. Your route drops steeply; watch your ankles here because the surface is uneven.

Above Tarr Steps

At the bottom of the field, go through a wooden five-bar gate. You'll see some stone ruins to your right, just as the path splits by a treed bank. Take the left-hand track, weaving its way down a steep field to the River Barle via a wooden gate. As previously mentioned, the water can be deep in places and the stones underneath the water slippery, so extreme care needs to be taken. It might be advisable to carry a towel, just in case you end up with wet feet!

When you reach the riverbank on the other side, locate the wooden five-bar gate leading into a field, signed 'Bridleway Tarr Steps'. Walking to the left of the river around the field, you'll eventually reach a wooden gate. Go through. It's a quiet stretch of path, with steep-sided woodland on the left. Arriving at a point where the path appears to split, carry on because the paths merge soon after.

At the next split, look for a wooden sign on the left and follow the path going left marked 'Bridleway Winsford Hill ½', climbing to a wooden gate – go through. When you hit another track, turn right for Winsford Hill, crossing a small ford before slipping immediately left. The path climbs steeply to another signpost, but it's not relevant to us because our route turns right. At a five-bar gate, go through and cross a field, keeping close to trees on the right. Just after a wooden gate on the right, you'll spot a smaller wooden gate ahead, on the roadside. Turn left and walk up the road to a cattle grid.

Enter the gate on the right of the cattle grid, turning right off the road, following the sign for 'Bridleway Winsford Hill ½, Knaplock 1'. When the stony track splits after some 18 m (20 yards), keep left. The track cuts through gorse bushes as it runs along the lower edge of Winsford Hill.

At a wooden sign in the centre of the track, turn right for 'Knaplock 1¾'. The path runs down to another sign. It may sound ominous but follow 'Bridleway avoiding bog'. It can get a bit wet, boggy and muddy, but stay close to the right-hand boundary; the route is indiscernible in places as it crosses open moorland frequented by Exmoor ponies.

Eventually, you'll reach a wooden five-bar gate with the blue bridleway mark. Go through and along the track flanked by a run of tree stumps on your left before turning into a wider, muddy track.

Another route joins from the left and the path splits but either option is okay because they rejoin, just as the track turns right and slips down to two gates. Bend left and go through the higher wooden gate and two further gates. At this point, walk down between farm buildings – this is Knaplock.

At the wooden sign, turn right for 'Bridleway Tarr Steps' into Watery Lane. As the name suggests, the track can become quite damp but look out for another of those ominous signs soon, informing you to turn to avoid the bog. Take the advice and head down over the field to a small wooden bridge crossing a stream. Once across, climb up to a five-bar gate. Go through and up the next field to another gate. Enter the field and, keeping snug to the left-hand boundary, walk up to a metal gate. Go into another field. Walk across to a further gate ahead.

In the following field, the path drops and runs between two enclosures before entering a further field and dropping quickly to Tarr Farm. A gate brings you out on to a road. Turn left and walk back up the road, keeping your eyes open for an entrance on the right, signed 'Permitted path for car park', returning you to your vehicle while avoiding the road.

DID YOU KNOW?

- The woods surrounding Tarr Steps were designated a National Nature Reserve in 2004. They are of importance internationally thanks to the mosses, lichens and liverworts. Found in burrows within the area, a type of moss seemingly glows in the dark.
- If you're a believer of local legend, then the clapper bridge was built by the devil who threatened to kill anyone using it. Matters were resolved when a courageous parson confronted the devil and reached a compromise.

WALK 23: *The Punchbowl – Winsford*

This pleasant walk starts high up on Exmoor, atop National Trust-managed Winsford Hill, a heath-blanketed common, and skirts the distinctive landform called The Punchbowl before descending and crossing a series of fields into the attractive village of Winsford, situated on the western bank of the River Exe.

For many, Winsford is the archetypal Exmoor village, with its thatched cottages, ancient inn, cosy tea garden, post office and river running by amid fields, hills and woods. The setting has understandably attracted its fair share of artists over the years, entranced by the natural beauty.

Turning back towards Winsford Hill, the route becomes wooded until it breaks out on to The Allotment, an open stretch

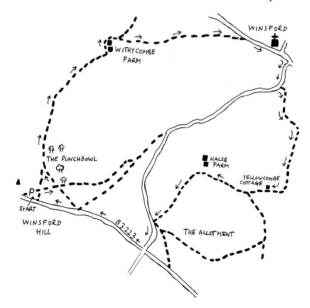

of grassland where, slightly off the route detailed below, one can find the inscribed Caractacus Stone, close to Spire Cross. One might argue it resembles a Neolithic Standing Stone but evidence suggests it dates from the post-Roman era. Caractacus was a well-known British chieftain who stood up to the Romans and marshalled the resistance to an invasion in AD 43.

Folklore is rife and various legends surround the stone: one tells the story of treasure buried underneath and an attempt by a local carter to retrieve it ending in disaster when the stone tumbled on to him; now, it's claimed, his ghost roams the area on foggy nights.

Once back on top of Winsford Hill, the walk to the car is along the verge of the picturesque B3223, although I recommend an extension to the detailed route in springtime, as described below, to see a blaze of colour within a popular bluebell wood.

Distance: 7.75 km/4¾ miles | Time: 2¼ hours | Parking and starting point: Travelling away from Exford on the B3223, look for a car park on the left marked by a post at the entrance, signalling 'Public bridleway Halse Lane ½' (grid ref: SS 878 341) | Toilets at start: None | Difficulties: There is a steady drop from the edge of The Punchbowl to Winsford and on the return leg a steep climb to the top of Winsford Hill | Map: Explorer map OL9

THE WALK

From the car park, follow in the direction of the marker post, stating 'Public bridleway – Halse Lane ½'. The route starts from a corner of the car park and cuts through swathes of heather, providing a beautiful blanket of colour when in bloom.

The path passes a little hollow on the right, with a solitary standing alone inside. A grassy, rutted track joins our path the right; our route bends left and around 27 m (30 yards)

Walking north-east, down around the edge of The Punchbowl, near Winsford

later, splits three ways. Select the middle path, heading downhill towards fields. You're now at the head of The Punchbowl.

Go straight ahead when a grassy path cuts across, although soon we'll join another grass track. Turn left, once you've taken a look into the Punchbowl's depths.

At a split, keep right, descending towards fields. It's a steady descent among scattered stunted trees and The Punchbowl on the right. Reaching a treed boundary and five-bar wooden gate, go through. You'll notice a blue-capped post at the wire fence. Walk down the field, keeping the fence close on the right.

Reaching another wire fence at the bottom of the field, go through the wooden gate in the right-hand corner, turning immediately left, marked on the signpost for Withycombe. Walk down the muddy, rutted track with a fence now close on the left, aiming for a farm.

As you reach the bottom, go through the larger five-bar gate, not the smaller one on the right, but not before turning around and admiring the view back into The Punchbowl; here, you can see it in all its splendour.

The Punchbowl, near Winsford

The rutted track bends around on itself and crosses Winn Brook via a wooden planked bridge before entering the farmyard of Withycombe Farm. As you pass barns and turn right, you'll see a yellow-marked wooden sign stating 'Bridleway – Ash Lane and Footpath – Winsford, turn right after next gate'.

We're heading for Winsford, so walk up the tarmaced road away from the farm and through a gate; just after, follow in the direction of the yellow-marked sign for 'Public footpath Winsford 1¼'. It's a grassy path running close to a wire and treed boundary,

with the road bending away to the left.

Soon, go through a five-bar wooden gate and carry on across a field to a gate, left of a telegraph pole. Go through and across the next field, keeping left of the treed boundary and a stream beyond.

Through another gate and straight on to a yellow-flagged kissing gate. Go through and across the field to a five-bar gate – and again. Go through the gate and straight across to another. Proceed straight across a further field, passing a yellow-marked telegraph pole, just

The village of Winsford

before kissing gates. Once through, follow a narrow, muddy path running close to trees on the right. Now, dwellings appear on your left, showing that you're approaching Winsford.

Over two stiles and you'll soon see rooftops and Winsford's church tower ahead. After the next stile, bend left and go through a wooden five-bar gate. You're now out on a narrow road, known as Ash Lane, so take care. Turn right and walk down the road, passing houses either side and the church (dedicated to St Mary Magdalene) on the left.

Cross a ford via the footbridge and you arrive in the centre of Winsford, with the quaint Bridge Cottage Tea Rooms and peaceful tea garden, immediately on your left. If you have your own sandwiches, a delightful picnic spot can be found over the small metal-railed bridge, next to the war memorial.

After you've finished exploring Winsford, begin the return stage of the walk by heading up Halse Lane, with the thatched Royal Oak Inn, a twelfth-century former farmhouse and dairy, on the left. Walk up the road, but just before it bends sharply right, take the track on the left, marked 'Winsford Hill 2½'. This

The village of Winsford

track, called Yellowcombe Lane, is also Dulverton and Tarr Steps-
bound.

When you reach a wooden gate on the left and a metal gate in
front of you, bend right and go up a narrow track, shaded by trees.
The stony path climbs and twists and eventually you'll notice a
spring running down on your left. On meeting a five-bar wooden
gate, just before the secluded Yellowcombe Cottage, go through.
Around 14 m (15 yards) later on the left, go over a blue-marked
stile and cross a footbridge.

At a wooden sign, follow for 'Bridleway to Summerway'. Ignore
a path on the left and continue ahead. At the next wooden sign,
cross the stream, turning right, marked 'Winsford Allotment', and
through the wooden gate on the other side of the spring. Cross
a small bridge by the cottage and turn left on to a stony path
leading up into woods. The path crosses a spring and continues
up through the woods.

When a path joins from the left, follow in the direction of
'Footpath Spire X [meaning Cross] ¾'. By some fallen trees, the
path crosses the spring and bends sharp right and then left, with

the first glimpses of Halse Farm ahead. Running alongside a wire fence, at the next wooden sign, follow 'Footpath to Folly', climbing up through the trees – mind where you step because tree roots protrude from the earth.

Finally, the path comes out from the trees and crosses a corner of grassland known as The Allotment. Another grass track joins from the left. Turn right towards a metal gate with a house on the right. Through the gate and choose the mud track ahead, bending slightly to the left before meeting a tarmaced road. Turn left, then right at the crossroads on to the B3223, in the direction of 'Exford 7/Withypool 6'.

Walk along the grass verge back to your car and enjoy open views along the way. The car park is on the right, nearly ¾ mile away.

If you want to extend the walk, *en route* to your car, look for a path on your right, around halfway between the crossroads and the car park. This eventually leads on to Halse Lane; but before reaching the lane cross to the left and into bluebell-strewn Burrow Wood, a perfect picture in springtime.

DID YOU KNOW?
- A local legend states that the distinctively-shaped Punchbowl was created by the devil.
- Labour politician Ernest Bevin, who died in 1951, was born in Winsford and lived the first eight years of his life there. The family house stands close to the present post office/shop.

Bluebells in Burrow Wood near Winsford Hill

Wimbleball Lake – Haddon Hill

On the eastern fringes of Exmoor, close to the town of Dulverton, lies Wimbleball Lake. Nestled in an upland valley surrounded by a varied landscape of woodland, farmland and heathland, it was built in the late 1970s; acting as a reservoir, it supplies water to West Somerset and many parts of Devon. But beyond its primary purpose, Wimbleball has become a popular destination for a host of activities, including fishing, sailing, cycling, walking and simply relaxing with a picnic while absorbing the atmosphere of this beautiful spot.

Much attention to detail has been afforded to the lake's development, such as the planting of over 12,000 trees native to Exmoor; the cover of woodland plus its other offerings attract wildlife and birdlife. The area is a draw for ornithologists, and among the species of bird on show are various members of the duck family, including pochard, widgeon and teal.

For anyone interested in circumnavigating the lake, it's a 13 km (8-mile) walk. Our route, however, takes us along the lake's south-western edge to a dam from where we climb to the Hadborough summit trig point (355 m/1,164 feet) and walk across Haddon Hill. From a visitors' car park, we drop down to the southern edge of Wimbleball and follow the lakeside walk back to the car park.

Haddon Hill, the biggest area of heathland on the Brendon Hills, boasts its own herd of Exmoor ponies – they've lived here since the 1970s. And such is the hill's importance, it's been designated not only a Special Area of Conservation (SAC) but a Site of Special Scientific Interest (SSSI), too. It's certainly a worthwhile area to explore during this walk – oh, and look out for the various willow sculptures along the lakeside, including a tree, whale and fisherman!

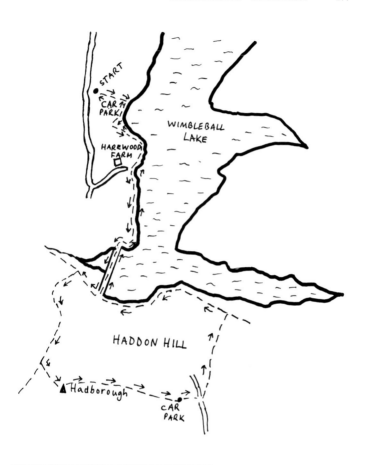

Distance: 7.25 km/4½ miles approx. | Time: 3 hours approx., with young children | Parking and starting point: The South West Lakes Trust pay-and-display car park at Wimbleball Lake (grid ref: SS 965 307) | Toilets at start: At the Visitor Centre in the car park | Difficulties: An easy walk with only one real climb on the way to the top of Haddon Hill | Map: Explorer map OL9

On the edge of Wimbleball Reservoir

THE WALK

From the car park in front of the tea shop, walk down the wide track signed for the play area until reaching the lakeside. You'll now see a sign for 'Woodland Discovery Trail'.

At the lake, turn right on to the Discovery Trail, also signed for the dam. Passing a wooden boathouse, the path bends right and left and goes through a wooden five-bar gate. Once through, turn left and go past the entrance to Wimbleball Sailing Club, joining a path for 'Lakeside Walk, Dam ¾ mile' and 'Woodland Discovery Trail'.

This permitted path runs to the right of the sailing club's fenced boundary and through another two wooden gates. All along, you're treated to lovely views of the lake – which is up to 50 m (164 feet) deep when full – and fields on the other side, stretching into the distance.

The path bends, following the shape of the reservoir, past the sailing club's wooden starting hut with views of West Hill Wood beyond, on the lake's eastern shore. The wood is an area of semi-

Cows chew the grass above Wimbleball Reservoir

natural deciduous woodland.

You'll pass a wooden shelter on the left before the path turns, skirting Harewood Farm and crossing a narrow wooden bridge.

Entering Eastern Wood, the path rises gently before veering around to the right and reaching the 50-m (164-foot) dam. It's worth stopping momentarily to check out the information board, explaining that the lake was formed by damming the River Haddeo. The construction began in November 1974 and it was some four years before the water supply was first used. The dam's design was selected to try and soften the overwhelming effects such a project inevitably has on its surrounding landscape. Much of the material, like the aggregate and sand, were sourced locally: Bampton and Cullompton respectively. The reason was that the pinkish tones of the materials would go some way to blending in with the immediate countryside.

Continue your walk by passing through the wooden gate and turning left on to the 300-m (985-foot) long dam, following the sign 'Permitted footpath Lady Harriet's Drive', with the lower slopes of Haddon Hill ahead of you.

Once across, turn right, signed 'Lady Harriet's Drive/Bury 2½'. The road, bordered both sides by trees, is named after Lady Harriet Acland (1749–1815), wife of Major John Dyke Acland. It's thought that she arranged for the drive to be built to connect her own estate with her daughter's.

At a wooden sign on the right, turn left on to the footpath for Haddon Hill. Climb the steep steps cut into the high stone wall. Go over a stile and go up through the trees.

When the trees begin to thin, you'll reach a stile. Go over and at a sign, at the edge of a track, follow the footpath to Haddon Hill, straight over the wide track, ignoring alternatives either side.

You'll climb up over the hillside via a narrow grassy path which twists up to a junction of faint paths. This isn't the clearest of routes and you'll have to pick your way at times.

Continue ahead at the junction before taking a very small path through ferns on your left, retaining a wider track to the right with lovely views beyond, down to Hartford Trout Farm and up over Hartford Wood to the village of Brompton Regis.

Walking on top Haddon Hill

When you notice a wider track on your left, almost adjacent to yours, join it and carry on up the slight incline. When the path splits, take the left-hand fork. Several faint paths make their way to the top and by now you should see the trig point ahead.

At the trig point, take a breather and admire the panoramic views. When you're ready, follow the exit shooting off in a north-easterly direction back to the wider track. Turn right. On your left, across the lake you'll spot the church at Upton.

Walk along the top of Haddon Hill until you approach a car park, hidden amongst trees. When the path splits three ways by the car park, ignore the left-hand split at right angles to your path as well as the right-hand path leading to a gate; instead, choose the middle route.

The path meets a tarmaced road. Turn right on to the road and after approx. 18 m (20 yards), turn left on to a path. Almost immediately on the left (around 8 yards past a black post), you'll see a faint path which becomes more discernible as it cuts down between shrubs and ferns.

Continue down until you reach a T-junction of paths. Turn right and then, after around 14 m (15 yards), left. Continue down through the woods to a wooden sign at a junction. Turn left, marked 'Bridleway to Dam and Bury'. Follow the bridleway until you see a stile down over on your right, just before a black wooden marker on the left.

Go over the stile, turn left and follow the narrow track, hugging the lakeside, back to the dam. Walk across and retrace your steps all the way to the car park.

DID YOU KNOW?

- Wimbleball Lake is the South West's biggest inland lake and boasts around 370 acres of water. Surrounding it are 500 acres of meadow and woodland.
- Haddon Hill is recognised for its importance to wildlife. Here, a colony of the endangered heath fritillary butterfly thrives.

WALK 25:   *Withypool Hill*

The tiny village of Withypool, high up on Exmoor, seems a world away from the hustle and bustle inextricably associated – it seems – with our modern lives. Here, the silence is almost palpable, the sense of tranquillity heightened by the mellifluous sound of the River Barle flowing under the village's impressive six-arched bridge. For around a century, the bridge has provided a route across the water, having replaced a packhorse variety which was sited further up the river.

The Barle cuts through the village, which gets its name from the myriad willow trees lining the banks. The lion's share of buildings are clustered around the water, including a general store-cum-post office, a seasonal tea room and the 300-year-old Royal Oak Inn.

This remote spot is surrounded by fields and open moorland and has many claims to fame – especially for such a small settlement. Take the Royal Oak Inn: not only did novelist R.D. Blackmore write part of his famous *Lorna Doone* while staying there, but Prince William dined with friends in 2006 while attending a nearby event; and that's not all: apparently, the 1930s saw the hostelry under the ownership of spymaster and, later, broadcaster Maxwell Knight and his wife, Gwladys.

Withypool is a fine base for walking, with popular routes following the river: in a westerly direction to the medieval Landacre Bridge and easterly to the ancient clapper bridge at Tarr Steps.

The walk I've chosen to feature, however, takes us south of the village to explore Withypool Hill, including a climb to its 398-m (1,305-foot) summit and a visit to an ancient stone circle, lying just a short distance from the cairn.

We'll begin with the walk's only real ascent – save for the short, steady climb to the cairn – as we head out of the village, but the climb is brief and we'll soon join the footpath rounding the

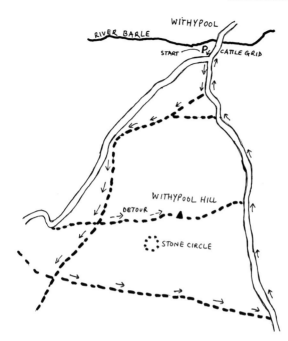

lower slopes of the hill. After a detour to the summit, we tackle the southern section of the hill before returning to Withypool.

It's a quiet walk and certainly not a honeypot route, even in the height of summer; plus, there is much upland scenery to admire.

_____

Distance: 5.25 km/3¼ miles approx. | Time: 1½ hours approx., with children and taking detour to cairn at the top of Withypool Hill | Parking and starting point: Small free car park in Withypool (grid ref: SS 844 354) | Toilets at start: Yes. From the car park, turn left and go over the cattle grid and bridge. Public toilets are on the right | Difficulties: No specific difficulties but a short ascent from the car park to the turning for the footpath at the beginning of the walk | Map: Explorer map OL9

THE WALK

Leaving the car park, turn right on to the road and walk up in the direction of Hawkridge, passing houses on the right. Continue up the steepening hill, passing Withypool Village Hall on the left at a sharp bend.

Look out for a wooden sign, signalling 'Restricted Byway Willingford Bridge 2½' on the right-hand side of the road. This is just under quarter of a mile from the car park.

Take this path, which boasts a lovely view on your right, down over the village, and on the left, up over the lower flank of Withypool Hill. As the path bends to the left and rises slightly, views across to barren Withypool Common appear.

You'll notice the path running close to the road heading from Withypool to South Molton and Sandy Way. When you reach three wooden posts on the left, with the road ahead, take a detour

RIGHT *Atop Withypool Hill*
BELOW *Walking eastwards around the southern end of Withypool Hill*

off the main track and wander up the narrower, unsigned left-hand path to the small cairn atop Withypool Hill; at a height of 398 m (1,305 feet), you'll be treated to fabulous views across one of Exmoor's more remote corners.

Before retracing your steps back to the lower path, take a moment to walk in a south-westerly direction to see the stone circle just below the hill top. These parts of the National Park have been inhabited since the Bronze Age, and around forty stones can

be spotted, although some are small and tricky to pinpoint; but it's an interesting site nonetheless and well worth experiencing.

Although the path you took up to the cairn is marked on the map as continuing the other side down to the road and the Exe Valley Way, which runs through this area, my suggested route returns on the same path, reaching the three wooden posts where you turn left.

At the next wooden sign, continue on the 'Restricted byway Willingford Bridge 2', branching left. Ignore a path later on the left and carry straight on, which climbs gently. At a crossroads of paths, continue ahead.

Nearly 183 m (200 yards) on the left, take the track with trees and a field to your right; another path will join yours from the left. After around a mile on this relatively straight path, which travels across the south of the hill, you'll meet a road (Worth Lane). Turn left and walk down the road.

As mentioned earlier, the Exe Valley Way uses this stretch of road into Withypool. This is the final stage of our walk, travelling back down the hill, passing the village hall and back to the car park, on the left before the cattle grid.

DID YOU KNOW?

- The Exe Valley Way can be split into ten easily manageable chunks, each taking around half a day to complete, making for an interesting long-distance walk for keen walkers.
- Apparently, General Eisenhower paid a visit to Withypool's Royal Oak Inn during his preparations for the D-Day landings. He was visiting troops based in the area; subsequently, he used the North Devon beach of Woolacombe, to the west, to replicate the French beaches.

WALK 26: *Withypool – Landacre Bridge*

This is a walk between two distinctive bridges, both spanning the River Barle with two miles of water flowing between them. Here, one feels at the true heart of Exmoor, a feeling accentuated by the open expanse of Withypool Common overlooking our walk from the south.

We begin in Withypool, from the village's six-arch stone bridge; we walk in a westerly direction, keeping close to the water which flows from its source on The Chains – a remote, desolate region of Exmoor – and reaches its confluence with the River Exe at Exebridge, Devon.

While Withypool's bridge dates back some hundred years or so, having been built to replace an old packhorse bridge further along the river, the five-arch Landacre Bridge, at which we arrive after our 2-mile riverbank stroll, dates back to medieval times.

Landacre is popular with tourists and locals alike, especially

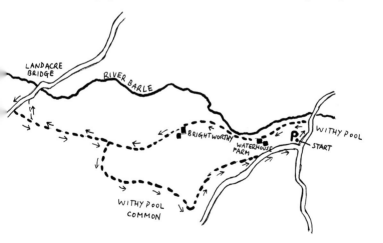

during the height of summer, when the open spaces are grabbed for picnics and children paddle in the rippling water.

The return leg of the walk finds us retracing our steps briefly before climbing up on to Withypool Common *en route* to our vehicle at the car pack in Withypool.

Distance: 7 km/4¼ miles approx. | Time: 2¼ hours approx. | Parking and starting point: Free car park in Withypool, close to the bridge (grid ref: SS 844 354) | Toilets at start: Near to the car park, just over the bridge before the café | Difficulties: No particular challenges, although there is a brief climb on the way back from Landacre Bridge, but nothing too strenuous | Map: Explorer map OL9

Withypool Bridge

THE WALK

From the car park, turn left and cross the cattle grid, bearing left before the bridge, following the sign for 'Landacre Bridge 2'. This gentle, level route follows the river west. After going through two wooden gates, you'll meet a stile. Once over, the path enters a field and moves a little further away from the river's course. Keep close to the field boundary and make for a wooden gate in the distance. Climb the stile, next to the gate, and carry on ahead.

You'll pass a large barn on your left, just before another gate and stile. Cross the stile and stay close to the left-hand field boundary.

Soon there is another stile, situated within a gap in a stone wall. Over the stile and turn right, following the sign for Landacre Bridge, 1¾ miles away.

Over a further stile and walk across a field, keeping tight to the wooden fence on your right; reaching the other end of the field, cross the stone footbridge and stile followed by a wooden footbridge.

By now, your path is, again, running along the water's edge and passes over another two wooden bridges before meeting a further stile. Hop over and continue to a wooden sign. Here, you'll need to head left, up over a field, marked 'Footpath to Landacre'.

Keep to the right of the field, close to trees and the river; there is a slight climb to a five-bar gate and stile. Once over, continue to another five-bar gate, passing farm barns on the left. By a farmhouse, follow the footpath sign and go through a five-bar gate or over the stile, positioned next to each other. Turning immediately left, keeping to the path bordered by wooden railings, you'll cross a wooden bridge and a further stile, before turning right for Landacre Bridge, now only a mile away.

You'll walk along a deep track shrouded by trees, giving welcome shade in summer, and pass a shelter on the right. Carry on ahead, ignoring a five-bar gate to the right. Go over another stile and straight ahead, remaining close to hedging on your right, to another five-bar gate. Go through and ignore the gate on the right, looking out for the yellow mark on top of a post, instead;

Looking west along the River Barle from Withypool

continue walking along the fenced boundary.

Through a five-bar gate and continue ahead, passing a sign informing you that the bridge is only ¼ mile. There are fine views on both sides now, across to fields on your right and up over the wide open moorland of Withypool Common to the left.

In places, the path isn't easily discernible but continue straight on, ignoring a faint left-hand split. Soon, Landacre Bridge comes into view. The path crosses a small stream before bearing right and running across to a pull-in for cars. As you meet a road, turn right and amble down to the bridge, a perfect spot for removing your flask and enjoying a few minutes' relaxation while listening to the Barle running along.

For the return leg of the walk, wander back up the road to a sign, marked 'Withypool 2'. This is the path you arrived on, so retrace your steps to a wooden gate where trees form a field boundary. Instead of going through, turn right just before and make your way up the side of the hill on to Withypool Common. Keep close to the field boundary on your left because the path itself isn't very apparent – it can also be muddy and marshy in places, especially after rainfall.

As the field boundary turns, the path becomes more obvious but remains close to the boundary. Now, views open out towards Withypool Hill and beyond.

Landacre Bridge

When the path splits, just past a five-bar gate on the left, keep walking ahead, ignoring a track heading off to the right. Cross over a small tarmaced track, leading down to Knighton, and carry on, staying close to the hedge, back towards Withypool.

When the field boundary ends, the path drops into a steep-sided combe. Cross the stream at the bottom of the combe and bear left.

Eventually, the path joins the road leaving Withypool and cuts across the moorland and Hawkridge Common. We don't want that direction so turn left, passing the entrance to Waterhouse Farm.

At the junction on arriving at Withypool, turn left and walk down to the car park, where you parked your car, some 37 m (40 yards) away on the left.

DID YOU KNOW?

- A nineteenth-century copy of *The National Gazetteer of Great Britain and Ireland* stated that Withypool was well known for a classic breed of small horned sheep and North Devon cattle.
- Next to a charming tea room, which had been an ironmonger's until around twenty years ago, are old-fashioned Shell petrol pumps. No longer in working order, they stand where an old garage existed.

Hawkridge – Anstey Gate

This walk runs close to the southern extremities of Exmoor National Park and, in fact, crosses the county border from Somerset into Devon *en route*.

Much of the walking takes place around and over West Anstey Common; the name, however, is rather deceptive because a glance at the OS map shows that it's actually a collection of commons, including Anstey Money Common, Woodland Common and Guphill Common.

The region, which has been used for military purposes in the past, has a long history in agricultural usage and is now Open Access land. Public bridleways and paths criss-cross a landscape where wild ponies hang out; this large swath of unenclosed

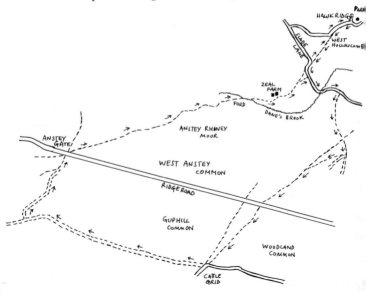

countryside typifies the beauty and remoteness of Exmoor's moorlands.

The walk begins in the quiet village of Hawkridge, high on Somerset's southern border, and for a time follows the Two Moors Way (see 'Introduction' for details on this long-distance walk).

Cutting up from the road on to the moorland of West Anstey Common, the route heads along the ridge before dropping to a delightful country lane running along the edge of the common. Then the walk climbs up to Anstey Gate and down over Anstey Rhiney Moor to Dane's Brook – rushing along to meet the River Barle. A ford is traversed via a series of stepping stones as you make your way back to Hawkridge.

Distance: 8.5 km/5¼ miles approx. | Time: 2¼ hours approx. | Parking and starting point: Roadside parking in the village of Hawkridge (grid ref: SS 860 306) | Toilets at start: None | Difficulties: No particular difficulties with plenty of easy walking. The early stages of the route involve walking along narrow roads, particularly Slade Lane, so take care | Map: Explorer map OL9

THE WALK

From the village of Hawkridge walk towards West Hollowcombe along a narrow road, taking care because there aren't any pavements. When you reach the entrance to West Hollowcombe, self-catering accommodation, on your left at a sharp bend, look for a wooden sign up the road alongside a gate on the left.

Go through, following in the direction of the public bridleway sign, indicating Slade Bridge is ½ mile away (0.8 km). Walk across the field, passing a small enclosed area on your left. You'll now follow the Two Moors Way for a time.

At the end of the field, go through the wooden gate and turn left. This is Slade Lane, again very narrow.

Ignore any footpath signs on the right, such as the one you'll pass as the road bends sharp left almost immediately. The road descends, passing the entrance to Zeal Farm on your right. Continue down to a cattle grid and Slade Bridge, under which Dane's Brook flows. As the sign informs you, you've just crossed the county border into Devon.

The 1:3 road climbs. Continue walking up until you notice a small wooden post, etched with a 'W', on the right, opposite a five-bar gate. Follow the narrow stony track taking you away from the road, signifying that you're still on the Two Moors Way.

The track, a permitted path, climbs up the hillside. Ignore any small turnings either side and carry on ahead when you see a relatively wide path cutting across your route.

Eventually, you'll reach a signpost, opposite a wooden five-bar gate, with the Two Moors Way continuing ahead, close to the left-hand boundary. Ignore another track ahead, too. Instead, bear right on to a narrow path and walk across Anstey Money

Looking north from West Anstey Common

Common while admiring the fine pastoral landscape beyond the common on your right.

Take no notice of paths on either side and continue until you finally meet Ridge Road. Cross and follow a track on the other side, signed 'Public Bridleway West Anstey 1½'. The path isn't clear and often it's a case of finding your way down over the common until meeting another road. A more defined path can be found a little further up, if you prefer.

On meeting the road, turn right and walk about 18 m (20 yards) to a road sign at a junction. Carry straight on, signed 'Ringcombe Farm only', disregarding the public bridleway to Hawkridge soon after on the right and other paths leading off in this direction.

Follow the tarmaced road for around 1.5 km (just under a mile); it's a quiet country lane and eventually passes Ringcombe Plantation, on the left, before bending left, crossing a cattle grid and continuing down to Ringcombe Farm. Before the cattle grid, our route carries on ahead along a wide stony track signed 'Bridleway Molland/Bremley'. Enjoy the views on the left down over fields to Combe Wood.

Go through a wooden five-bar gate and look for a wide, unsigned track on the right which bends and climbs to Anstey Gate on the ridge of the common. Cross a cattle grid and at the wooden signpost join the public bridleway for 'Hawkridge 1½'. There is another path adjacent to it, but your route is on the left, turning away from the road.

The track makes its way down over Anstey Rhiney Moor. Again, ignore any paths off or which cut across your route. Sometimes, the route isn't particularly clear and seems to disappear for short stretches occasionally. Ultimately, you'll reach a ford – this is Dane's Brook.

There is a signpost at the edge of the ford. Use the stepping-stones to cross, travelling in the direction of 'Bridleway – Hawkridge 1 (Deep Ford)'. Most times it isn't a problem crossing the water via the stones, but if you prefer to avoid it, turn right before the water's edge and walk in the direction of 'Permitted

Walking down over Anstey Rhiney Moor

footpath to Slade Bridge Avoiding Ford'.

Once across the ford, go through the five-bar wooden gate and continue up through the trees. Go through the metal gate leading into the grounds of Zeal Farm and walk up towards the farmhouse; go through the white gate. Turn right and through another gate. A wooden signpost on your left directs you on to a public bridleway up over a field; there are glorious views on the right across to East Anstey Common.

Go through a wooden five-bar gate with the splash of blue signifying public bridleway. Then, cross the next field, keeping close to the right-hand boundary. By a stone barn in the right-hand corner of the field, you'll see a metal gate by a wooden sign.

Go through and turn left on to Slade Lane, which you walked down at the start of the walk.

Head up the road. As it bends right and immediately left, turn off on the second bend, through a wooden gate, signed 'MW Public Bridleway Hawkridge ½'. Cross the field, passing the small fenced off area in the middle. Soon, house roofs appear. Head to the left of the first one you see. You'll reach a wooden five-bar gate. Go through and out on to the road, just by the sharp left bend and a wooden carved bench on the right.

Walk down the road, passing West Hollowcombe on the right. Before long, you'll be back in Hawkridge, where you left your car.

DID YOU KNOW?
- It's thought that the name Anstey means 'narrow path', a reference perhaps to the Bronze Age ridgeway running across the common.
- The church at Hawkridge has a Norman doorway and font.

Exmoor ponies on Anstey Rhiney Moor

WALK 28: *Larkbarrow – Badgworthy Hill – Great Ashcombe*

This walk is not only the longest featured in this book but includes the most gruelling section, too. And that's largely because of walking across deep grassy moorland with no recognisable path and, in particular, the drop from Great Ashcombe to Warren Bridge. It's very steep with, again, no discernible path down over an uneven, tussocky terrain full of pits – it's real hard graft and explains why there is a rather blunt message on a sign stating: 'Very arduous, steep and muddy'.

That aside, this is a walk highlighting just one aspect of the National Park's landscape: apart from areas like The Chains, this is wild and remote Exmoor at its best. Few trees, rolling, grassy, barren moorland, deep valleys, streams – even an isolated ruin.

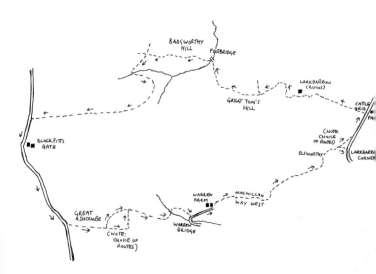

Once a Victorian farmstead, Larkbarrow – which takes its name from a Bronze Age burial mound which has virtually disappeared at Larkbarrow Corner – was used for target practice during the Second World War. Here, at 1,200 feet above sea level, tragedy struck when in 1923, Will Little, one of the residents, was struck by lightning during a fierce storm. He'd been working at nearby Warren Farm and was wending his way home when the incident happened.

But Larkbarrow is relatively early in the walk which drops down into Badgworthy Valley before climbing around Badgworthy Hill and, later, across grassy moorland to the B3223. The toughest segment of the walk occurs on the return leg so tread carefully.

Distance: 19 km/12 miles approx. | Time: 5½ hours approx. Parking and starting point: Park in the small lay-by close to a cattle grid (grid ref: SS 835 422) | Toilets at start: None | Difficulties: This is the longest walk in the book and, at times, the most challenging. For many stretches of the route there are no clear paths so you will be making your way across a relatively featureless landscape. The descent from Great Ashcombe to Warren Bridge is extremely arduous and requires care because the surface is steep and uneven. This route is best walked on a clear, dry day – don't pick a foggy one | Map: Explorer map OL9

THE WALK

After parking your car near the cattle grid, go through the gate in the direction of the sign, 'Public bridleway Badgworthy Valley 3½, Malmsmead 6'.

Walk to a small wooden gate. Go through and turn right, signed 'Badgworthy Valley 2½, Oare 4½, Oareford 3¾'. Next, you'll reach a large wooden gate after which you'll continue following the bridleway sign.

It's a decent wide track which runs along the wired boundary

TOP *Low-lying mist in the distance near Larkbarrow*
ABOVE *The remains of Larkbarrow, a farm used for target practice during the Second World War*

on your left. On the right, look out for the ruins of Larkbarrow, just before a five-bar gate. Once through, the wired boundary is on your right. Go through another five-bar gate.

The path continues to hug the fenced boundary, eventually bending right. Follow it to another wooden five-bar gate. Go

A lonely sheep near Larkbarrow

through. You'll pass a wooden signpost on your right – just before a ruined wall – pointing across to the left for 'Public bridleway Warren Farm'. Ignore this.

Reaching a wooden five-bar gate and signpost named Edward's Post, take the permitted path for Badgworthy Valley and Malmsmead. This is a remote, barren corner, a wild untamed part of Exmoor where few trees or shrubs exist, just an undulating grass-clad landscape which tests your navigational skills if the mist comes down.

The path sweeps across Great Tom's Hill and arrives at a small wooden gate with a signpost on the right. Go through and follow the path for Badgworthy Valley, cutting down on the left, just inside the gate – again a permitted path.

You'll drop down into the valley and see a small path joining on the left, just before crossing a trickle of water, after which the path climbs briefly. Ignore a small path running off to the left and continue down to a footbridge crossing Badgworthy Water. Go over the bridge and through the wooden gate, before turning left and climbing up a narrow path. You'll see Hoccombe Water, near its confluence with Badgworthy Water, down on your left as you climb around the contours of Badgworthy Hill.

The grassy terrain around the side of Badgworthy Hill

Eventually, you'll see a grassy track coming down from the right and running across your path before carrying on down towards the water. It's not particularly clear but take this route and cross the water. Go through a wooden gate with a signpost on the left stating, 'Bridleway B3223'. It's a steep climb with the path bending to the west as it heads towards the B3223. The stony path ends and a sea of grass opens out in front of you. Getting to the road is a case of making your way across this Open Access land because there is no path – and it's like that for around 3 km (2 miles), too.

When you reach the boundary next to the B3223, look for the wooden five-bar gate and a stile alongside, which gets you over the fence and on to the road. The wooden signpost next to the gate is pointing back towards Badgworthy Valley so is irrelevant.

Turn left on the road and walk along the grass verge where possible. You'll pass a field on the right where mire restoration is taking place. Mires – peat accumulating habitats, including fens and blanket bogs – are globally scarce with various actions, such as moorland reclamation, compounding the problem. Over the centuries, Exmoor has been affected with its supply of blanket bogs and peat drying out which has, therefore, impacted the wildlife and plants. After a pilot study, the Exmoor Mire Restoration Project was launched in 2006 to help restore this fragile element of the landscape.

Continue down the road, passing a house and smallholding on the left, before bending left over a small road bridge. Carry on along that road, past a lay-by-cum-car park on the right, opposite Prayway Meads. There are fine open views on the left all along this road.

When you reach Great Ashcombe on the left, go through a wooden gate and keep close to the hedged boundary on the right. Both the Two Moors Way and Macmillan Way West follow this route, before the former drops south to Simonsbath. You remain on the Macmillan Way West for a while as you cross open land, passing a barn.

When you reach a signpost by a metal gate, continue in the direction of 'Warren Drive 1¾'. At a gate, with a field boundary ahead of you, turn left and follow the boundary down to a small gate; alternatively, before this, you can follow the Macmillan Way West, which isn't signed so check your OS map, around to a small wooden gate further down in the valley.

Whatever route you take, once you're through there is a very challenging and gruelling drop to a boundary at the valley floor. It's wet, very steep, long grass, pitted – and there is no path. The sign at the water's edge warns those going up that they're in for a tough time: the notice should be replicated and placed at the top, too.

Cross the River Exe in the direction of the footpath. Over a stile and turn left, walking up through the gap in the treed boundary, some 18 m (20 yards) away. Head up the field for a short distance and join the footpath taking you to a gate at the edge of a tarmaced road. Go through, with Warren Bridge to the right.

Turn left and start a steady climb up the road, which bends left around Warren Farm. Look for the large metal gate on the right, with the left-hand post marked with the 'MAC' (Macmillan Way

West) sign and on the right a signpost showing 'Public bridleway Larkbarrow Corner 2'. Go through and follow the wide track.

Pass through a metal and two wooden gates. Eventually, you'll pass a wooden sign on the right of the track, by a spring, pointing left for 'Permitted bridleway Larkbarrow'. Ignore this and continue ahead; now it's a case of making your way across the open grassland of Elsworthy.

As you approach a fenced boundary in front of you, head for the five-bar gate in the corner. As soon as you go through, the path splits. Here, you have two options: either you can pick the right-hand path to Larkbarrow Corner. On reaching the road, turn left and walk up to the cattle grid and your car, some 1.5 km (1 mile) away. Alternatively, back at the split after the gate, carry on ahead and stay off the road a little longer. When the track splits further along, keep right. Eventually, you'll see a fenced enclosure by the boundary. Go through the wooden gate on to the road. Turn left and, again, walk up the road to your car by the cattle grid.

DID YOU KNOW?

- It's believed that the bridleway running from Warren Farm across Elsworthy to Larkbarrow Corner was to be the site of a railway line running from Simonsbath to Porlock Weir. Planned by John Knight in the 1820s, it was never completed.

- In 2008 archaeologists from Exmoor National Park, assisted by volunteers, visited the abandoned Victorian farm ruins at Larkbarrow with the aim of confirming the date of prehistoric activity which had occurred on the site. Flint had been found back in the 1950s. It was established later that activities took place between 8000–4000 BC.

WALK 29:   *Roadwater – Chidgley – Nettlecombe*

Tucked away in a deep wooded valley, the village of Roadwater is best known for its associations with the West Somerset Mineral Line. It's long gone, of course, but this 18-km (11-mile) railway, built between 1857–64, played a pivotal role in local industry. Along the tracks, iron ore was carried from mines up in the Brendon Hills to the Bristol Channel port of Watchet. A year later, in 1865, it opened to passenger traffic. Although this walk doesn't actually set foot on the route, which has in recent years been preserved – minus the tracks – for people to enjoy, you're never far from it during the early stage of the walk.

From Roadwater, we cover a stretch of the 58-km (36-mile) Coleridge Way, named after the Romantic poet, Samuel Taylor Coleridge (see 'Introduction' for details of this long-distance walk).

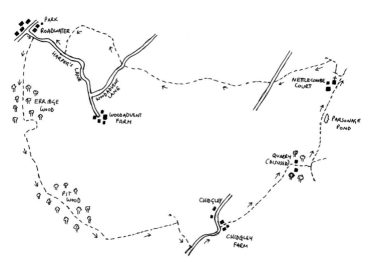

Woods, valleys, pastures are among some of the delights we experience on a route which takes us to the impressive Nettlecombe Court, a grand mansion hidden in a secluded valley. Originally a manor house, it served as a girls' boarding school in the 1960s before, in 1967, becoming a field centre. Next to the house stands the Church of St Mary the Virgin.

Leaving the mansion behind, the route climbs and runs down through fields all the way back to our starting point in Roadwater, with views of the Brendon Hills and across to the region's northern coastline to enjoy.

Distance: 9 km/5½ miles approx. | Time: 3 hours approx. | Parking and starting point: Roadside parking in the village of Roadwater (grid ref: ST 031 382) | Toilets at start: None | Difficulties: There are some rises to contend with but much of this walk is easy; there are short patches, though, which can become overgrown, particularly during the growing season | Map: Explorer map OL9

THE WALK

On leaving your car, you need to locate Harper's Lane. Although no road sign is present, a blue sign advising 'Road Ahead Narrows to 9ft Width' stands at its junction with the main road. You'll also see a property named The Old Bakery on the left upon entering the road: this was the site of the village bakery until the 1950s when it was converted into a residential dwelling.

Go past a no-through road sign on the right, signed 'Mineral Line', and continue up the hill. Around a bend, you'll need to turn right off the road, marked 'Public bridleway to Sticklepath'.

Pass through a wooden five-bar gate and on to a grass track running along the bottom of a steep field. Soon, you'll reach a small wooden five-bar gate; go through and into Erridge Wood, a dense patch of woodland.

After around 500 m (⅓ mile), the path drops and bends sharp left just before a small clearing. At a wooden gate, go through and across the field, over a spring and turn right to another wooden gate. Once through, you're back in the woods for a short time.

After another small wooden gate, you'll leave the trees behind and continue along part of the Coleridge Way. At a crossroads of paths, ignore the left-hand route up over a field and the right-hand option down to the Mineral Line. Instead, carry on ahead with the path running up against a fence on your right.

Ignore two turnings into a field past some houses and carry on into Pit Wood. At a wooden gate, go through. Ignore a sign on the left of the path, pointing down through trees on the right to the Mineral Line. Around 18 m (20 yards) later, at another wooden sign, head in the direction of 'Bridleway to Sticklepath 1½'. You'll be faced with two paths facing you – choose the one ascending and identified by a blue bridleway mark on a tree.

Ignore an unsigned path bending sharp left. Carry on and go through a wooden gate. You're still on the Coleridge Way and to your right there are beautiful views encompassing pastures, fields

Walking towards Nettlecombe Court

and woodland along this valley route.

Eventually, you'll reach a large five-bar gate at the end of a field. Go through and at the wooden signpost, turn right for 'Public footpath B3190, Sticklepath ¼'. The relatively enclosed narrow path runs between trees and bushes to a metal gate. Once through, you're on the road so watch your step.

Turn left and walk along the road. When it bends sharp left, look for the Royal Mail letterbox against a wall on the right, next to a sign for Chidgley Farm. Alongside, you'll see a wooden sign showing 'Footpath Nettlecombe 1 (through gate)'. The gate in question looks more like an entrance to a garden and is located at the other end of a tarmaced parking area.

Beyond the gate, walk along the track, which bends left, up to two metal gates. Ignore the first gate, on the right, and go through the one in front of you. The grassy track runs along the foot of a steep field with a wire boundary on the left.

Eventually, you'll reach a metal gate. Enter and walk straight across a field, aiming for the bottom right corner where you'll see two wooden stiles next to two gates. This area was overgrown with

Nettlecombe Court and church

nettles and weeds when I last walked it so take care if you don't want to be stung. Once over the stiles, the footpath clings to the left-hand boundary; again, this stretch isn't the best maintained along the route and I had to negotiate some fallen trees and nettles.

Once you've got past this overgrown stretch, you'll arrive at a wooden gate. Go through and pass a stone barn on the left. Follow the footpath sign and cross a yard with a house on the right. Walk up to another wooden sign, just before the track bends right. Keep left, heading for Nettlecombe. Don't go over the wooden stile, that route takes you to nearby Monksilver.

The path runs along the edge of a field and reaches a wooden gate close to a metal gate. Go through both and continue. Soon, you'll pass Parsonage Pond on the right, just as you approach Nettlecombe Court, the Leonard Wills Field Centre.

On reaching the Court, go through the black metal gate. The gravel track bends round to the Court and church, which stands alongside. You need to keep close to the black metal railings on the right, walking straight on and out through the entrance flanked by two pillars with horse busts atop.

The rural landscape of the Brendon Hills

Looking across fields to the Bristol Channel

Turn first left on to a tarmaced lane, which passes the church and bends right and left. Go by a building on the right with a large arched entrance. The track climbs to a split. Go straight on, through a wooden five-bar gate, following the public bridleway sign.

No longer tarmaced, the track climbs. You'll notice a wooden sign on the left, opposite a damaged tree trunk. Turn left in the direction of 'Roadwater 2½'. Go through a five-bar gate and up over a steep field.

At the top, ignore a small wooden gate in the left-hand corner and walk on to the next gate. Go through and over a rough patch of ground with no marked path for a few metres to a stile on the right. Over the stile, following the sign for 'Public footpath Roadwater 1½' which crosses a narrow track and continues ahead. When the path splits, carry straight on.

On reaching a metal gate, go through and across a field, keeping high. Over a stile and across the next field, again staying high, close to a hedge on your left. At the end of this field, go over another stile, following the sign for 'Roadwater 1'.

At the bottom of the field, pass through a field entrance/exit with a yellow-capped post alongside. Follow the track down over the next field and through a gate on to Woodadvent Lane. Take care crossing this narrow lane. You'll see a signpost by the gate for 'Public footpath Roadwater ¼', directing you through another field.

Cross in a diagonal direction. As the land drops away steeply, look for an exit in the bottom corner, close to trees. Go over two stiles, following the Roadwater footpath. Down the next field and over the stile in the bottom left-hand corner. Once over, follow the field around to the right and through an ungated entrance. At this point, turn immediately left. The narrow path runs up against the boundary and can, again, become overgrown.

At the end of the path, go over another stile on to Harper's Lane. Turn right and walk down the road, eventually passing ground covered at the start of the walk. You'll see the Old Bakery on the right, just before the main road. Return to your car.

DID YOU KNOW?

- Poet Samuel Coleridge moved to the village of Nether Stowey in 1797. He was an avid walker and the Coleridge Way covers the routes along which he enjoyed wandering.

The village of Roadwater

Dulverton is deemed the southern gateway to Exmoor National Park. It's a busy little town positioned alongside the River Barle at a point where the deep and wooded valley opens out on nearing its confluence with the Exe.

The road bridge spanning the Barle at the southern end of town is an attraction in itself. This five-arched construction dates from medieval times but has been upgraded on several occasions over the centuries.

Other attractions include the Church of All Saints, one of two churches in Dulverton, with this Grade II listed building boasting a fifteenth-century tower. The market house, in the heart of town, dates from the mid-eighteenth century and was converted into a town hall a century later.

It's arguably the remotest town on Exmoor and as such exudes a feeling of self-sufficiency: walking around its streets you pass a range of shops catering for locals and visitors alike.

This walk begins in the town, crosses the Barle and heads in a westerly direction, leaving the houses and shops behind to explore a largely agricultural landscape of fields and meadows. It's a quiet, peaceful walk which won't take too long, therefore allowing you plenty of time to explore the town before returning to your car.

Distance: 5.5 km/3½ miles approx. | Time: 1¾ hours approx. | Parking and starting point: Roadside parking or pay-and-display car parks in Dulverton (grid ref: SS 913 278) | Toilets at start: At the car parks | Difficulties: A few climbs up over fields but not a particularly challenging walk | Map: Explorer map OL9

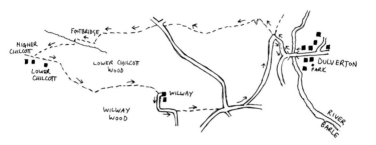

THE WALK

From your car, walk along Bridge Street and cross Dulverton Bridge, alias Barle Bridge, leaving the town centre behind. On the right, immediately after crossing the bridge, turn into Oldberry Lane. Follow in the direction of 'Public footpath Beech Tree Cross 1½, Hawkridge 4½'.

Dulverton Church

When you reach a junction on a sharp left bend, turn right passing a no-through road sign and footpath sign. At the next sign at a split, bear right on to the public footpath. At a further split, close to a white cottage, bear left for 'Beech Tree Cross 1'. Join a narrow path climbing up through the woods, zig-zagging to a wooden gate.

Go through and emerge from the trees into a field. Keep close to the right-hand boundary, heading in the direction of Beech Tree Cross, now only ½ mile away.

Walk up over the field to a metal gate. Go through, cross a tarmaced track (leading down to Old Berry Farm) and pass through the small wooden gate opposite. Stroll down over the field, passing a wooden waymark in the centre. At the boundary,

Down over fields west of Dulverton

go over the stile (or through the wooden gate) into the next field.

Keep high, close to the left-hand treed boundary. Head across the field before descending to the bottom right-hand corner, crossing a stile. Be careful: after the stile, the ground drops away abruptly on to a tarmaced road.

Turn right on to the road and walk some 55 m (60 yards) to a post indicating a footpath alongside a metal gate. Enter and drop down over the field, passing a wooden waymark (it had collapsed when I last completed the walk).

Reaching the bottom of the field, you'll see a cluster of trees by a spring. The wooden gate opposite carries the yellow-arrowed footpath plaque. Go through and turn left.

Walk along the lower section of this steep field before gradually climbing across and walking around the far side, close to the trees and stream on the left.

Look for a small wooden footbridge amongst the trees. Cross, walk up a brief incline and then turn right, following a grassy path along the bottom of the field. At the corner, the route turns right and ascends, again staying close to the treed boundary, before passing through a wooden gate into another field.

Once through, turn right and go through a small wooden gate. Cross the next field to a metal gate, hidden slightly by trees, in the far corner. Pass through and turn left on to the unsigned Chilcott Lane which narrows just past a gate.

As you approach a wooden gate in front of you, bear right in the direction of the small footpath plaque on the gate post. This stretch, like others along the route, can become muddy after rainfall.

The path runs between two fields, canopied by trees. At a dilapidated metal gate, go through, again following the yellow footpath arrow. This point was very overgrown on my last visit and negotiating plenty of nettles was required.

This is a steep field so keep high as you walk over to a metal gate at the far end; turn left once through into the next field, strolling close to the boundary and up to a waymark before dropping down to a metal gate. Water running past the gate is a recipe for muddiness, so be prepared!

Walk up the next steep field and through a metal gate on to a path rising gradually to a narrow tarmaced track. Go past the entrance to Wilway (a house with outbuildings) and walk along the track which turns sharp left – take care. Just before it bends right, go through a metal gate marked with the footpath arrow on the right-hand post.

Keep tight to the hedge on the left as you walk across the field. Go through another metal gate, down over the next field to a further gate, after which you join a road with a bungalow on the left.

Walk along the road, passing a green Exmoor National Park

Old cottages in Dulverton

sign on the left, just before a junction. Don't turn left towards Hawkridge; instead, continue straight ahead signed 'Dulverton ½'. When you reach another turning on the left, opposite an entrance to a dwelling named Barnfield, turn into the road, marked by a blue cycle route sign.

Walk down the narrow road, which bends sharp right by a house and turning on the left, until you reach the B3222 crossing Dulverton Bridge. Walk back to your car but not before taking time to explore the town.

DID YOU KNOW?

- Sir George Williams, who founded the YMCA, was born further up the River Barle at Ashway Farm in 1821.
- The National Park Authority is based at Exmoor House, close to the town's medieval bridge, in a building which was once the workhouse.

TOURIST INFORMATION CENTRES AND NATIONAL PARK CENTRES

EXMOOR NATIONAL PARK CENTRES

Dunster
Dunster Steep, Dunster, Somerset
TA24 6SE
Tel: 01643 821835; email:
NPCDunster@exmoor-
nationalpark.gov.uk

Dulverton
7-9 Fore Street, Dulverton,
Somerset TA22 9EX
Tel: 01398 323841; email:
NPCDulverton@exmoor-
nationalpark.gov.uk

Lynmouth
Lyndale Car Park, Lynmouth,
Devon EX35 6EX
(this is a temporary location
while the usual base is being
refurbished)
Tel: 01598 752509; email:
NPCLynmouth@exmoor-
nationalpark.gov.uk

TOURIST INFORMATION CENTRES

Combe Martin
Seacot, 13 Cross Street, Combe
Martin, Devon EX34 0DH
Tel: 01271 883319

Lynton and Lynmouth
Town Hall, Lee Road, Lynton,
Devon EX35 6BT
Tel: 01598 752225

Minehead
West Somerset Visitor Centre,
Warren Road, Minehead,
Somerset TA24 5BG
Tel: 01643 702624

South Molton
1 East Street, South Molton,
Devon EX36 3BU
Tel: 01769 574122

OTHER TOURISM OFFICES

Porlock
Porlock Visitor Centre, West End,
Porlock, Somerset
Tel: 01643 863150

Watchet
Watchet Tourist Office, 8 The
Esplanade, Watchet, Somerset
TA23 0AJ
Tel: 01984 632101

USEFUL CONTACTS

Exmoor National Park
Exmoor House, Dulverton,
 Somerset TA22 9HL
 Tel: 01398 323665; www.
 exmoor-nationalpark.gov.uk

Holnicote Estate
(owned and managed by the
 National Trust)
 Selworthy, Somerset TA24 8TJ
 Tel: 01643 862452

Traveline
(Bus & rail travel enquiry line for
 South West)
 Tel: 0871 200 2233; www.
 traveline.org.uk

West Somerset Railway
Tel: 01643 704996; www.west-
 somerset-railway.co.uk

The National Trust
PO Box 39, Warrington, Cheshire
 WA5 7WD
 Tel: 0844 800 1895; www.
 nationaltrust.org.uk

Dunster Castle
Dunster, Somerset TA24 6SL
 Tel: 01643 823004 (information
 line)

Natural England
1 East Parade, Sheffield S1 2ET
 Tel: 0845 600 3078; www.
 naturalengland.org.uk

USEFUL SOURCES OF INFORMATION

The following books, pamphlets
and websites are useful sources
of information on all matters
Exmoor.

BOOKS

Enjoying Exmoor (Exmoor
National Park Authority,
Dulverton, 1985, ISBN:
0861830725)

Exmoor National Park by Glyn
Court (Webb & Bower
Ltd, Exeter, 1987, ISBN:
0863501419)

*Exmoor: The Official National Park
Guide* by Brian Pearce (Pevensey
Guides, Newton Abbot, 2001,
ISBN: 1898630151)

PAMPHLET

*Explore Holnicote: Exmoor National
Park* by The National Trust

WEBSITES

www.everythingexmoor.org.uk
www.exmoor-nationalpark.gov.uk
www.wikipedia.org

INDEX